Beyond Forgotten Veils

An engaging look at one prodigal son's spiritual journey Home

*To Hal
Hope this helps you
to discern Truth from
illusion
Ray*

Raymond Pratt

Outskirts Press, Inc.
Denver, Colorado

Beyond Forgotten Veils
An engaging look at one prodigal son's spiritual journey Home

Outskirts Press, Inc.
http://www.outskirtspress.com

ISBN: 978-1-4327-1486-4

Outskirts Press and the "OP" logo are trademarks belonging to Outskirts Press, Inc.

PRINTED IN THE UNITED STATES OF AMERICA

Dedications

This book is dedicated to the Third Person of the Holy Trinity, namely

The Holy Spirit.

It is also dedicated to my mother, Marie, my ex-wife, Cristina and all of my children, Ciaran, Cristin, Brendan, Brian, Cathal and Conor.

WITHOUT ANY OF THEM THIS BOOK WOULD NEVER HAVE BEEN COMPLETED

Thank you all!

** Author's photograph taken by Mr. Carl Oelerich

BROTHERS AND SISTERS

I give you to the Holy Spirit as part of myself,

I know that you will be released

Unless I want to use you to imprison myself.

In the name of my freedom I choose your release,

Because I recognize that we will be released

Together.

From the *A Course in Miracles*

Table of Contents

Prologue

When I was a little boy, growing up in Ireland in the nineteen fifties and sixties, one of the most important achievements for me was my becoming an altar boy. There must have existed something deep within me of a vaguely atavistic nature about my being able to gleefully swing the large and heavily gilded silver thurible during our religious services. Swinging it to and fro during the afternoon Benediction service was my constant joy, as the whole church filled with vast and fragrant cumulus-like clouds of the rare sweet frankincense. During those very same latent but precarious "affirmations of faith," it was Church Latin that I would quickly learn, thus finally becoming the 'lingua franca' of my youthful faith.

This would also lead me on my first steps into the limitless world of foreign languages, which would have to include the Irish Gaelic (Gaeilge), our own exotic and original national language. The Gaelic was compulsory for us to learn within the framework of the other general subjects that we were taught, if we were ever going to consider the thought of ultimately redeeming our high school diplomas (Irish, scrudu ardteistimearachta). Oddly enough, both languages, the Gaelic and Latin, in all honesty could be classified as "dead as dodo" languages, but both would play a particularly important role later on in my life in their own subtle way. Moreover in a way that would whet an insatiable appetite for true knowledge and that would instill within me a profound fondness of learning.

Understanding old languages apparently helps us to get a clearer picture of any given subject at hand and is necessary when trying to relate some stories that do entail 2,000-year-old personalities. I have endeavored to include into my own studies, and all for the sake of this book's integrity, the occasional foreign word or word structure in the effort to keep to their true meaning. This is done so to the very best of my ability for I do not have any express intention or secret agenda in trying to alter anyone's belief system. I find that the positive changes in this particular area can only come from inside, and it is then that one's heart is open to the Holy Spirit, or if you wish, the Voice within. For that matter, I am inclined to believe that this first book of mine was written with more than just a little help from above and I will tell you why.

After surviving the rigors of an extremely traumatic divorce, I am certain that everyone involved needed healing, and all of the members of my family did undoubtedly suffer to various degrees. It was also to be during this period that I found a little time to analyze our interconnected lives. During this 'dark night of the soul' time, approximately one to three years after my divorce, I found this, perhaps, to be the most intense period of my life, stirring up forceful passions and sentiments that might have been better off left alone. In comparison to the few other traumatic events that I have been unfortunate to occasion, I found myself not very well seasoned for this, my most dangerous interlude.

I made a brave and sincere effort to contend with my ongoing heartbreak. This I did by instigating some 'corporal works of mercy' and without any particular commentary I found that they could but only help me significantly. This would include a short eye-opening teaching visit to a young female offender's prison, a very moving but fulfilling encounter. I also started to teach the various popular New Age subjects to relatively small but compact classes and it was during this time that I was introduced to a book that would change my life's direction. This now well-known book that I refer to was Gary Renard's superbly readable accounts called *The Disappearance of the Universe*, a must for any dedicated spiritual wayfarer. Gary also followed up on his first successful book with another that he has called *Your Immortal Reality*, which tends to enhance all of what he has already written.

However, this first book of Gary's would point me in the direction of another absolutely amazing and truly compelling spiritual book, and this would be *A Course in Miracles*. Oddly enough, it was that very same book, the following day, I would find lying on my dining room table, a thoughtful and kindly thank-you gift from Linda, my sister in Texas. This to me was beginning to look like the work of higher powers, most probably the Holy Spirit's Call, and thus initiated me on my own personal quest.

Within this humble book, you may see an outline given in no particular order of some indirect paths that I have taken that have led me to forgiving. For so many, it would seem, needed to be recognized, forgiven, and released, and the list I had, when perfunctorily screened, looked unending. There was always going to be my foes perceived in the wrong light, my ex-wife (no minor feat) and her allies. There were my children (of which I have five boys and one girl), many of whom did not want, nor still wish to this day, any type of connection with me so far. Children, God bless them, they do tend from their hurts to be so uncompromising in their young hearts, but we must then be unconditional and totally loving in forgiving them. However, all this would finally culminate with a very important decision that generally people find particularly hard to do. Yet this was to be the hardest thing for me to accomplish in finding closure; it was the need to forgive myself.

For it was only then that I understood something of paramount importance to me. If I had not gone through the living hell that divorce relentlessly brings, I would, most probably, NOT be writing a prologue for my book today. In fact this book I that I have written, under more auspicious circumstances, might not ever have been completed. This also led me to believe in the following possibility, the possibility that this whole situation may have all been scripted and put together at a completely different, if not necessarily a higher level. I do believe implicitly that the Holy Spirit takes that which we have no need of, and turns it into something He can distinctly use for us!

This book is simply about the use of forgiveness in a more advanced form. It is simply about finding a way through the smoke and mirrors, flotsam and jetsam that seem to pervade our everyday lives. Through the use of *A Course in Miracles*, I try to give you some insight into what is important and what is not and how it can subtly change a way of thinking that may have reached stasis or even stagnation. All the books here that I have mentioned should become part of your final quest.

Moreover, in the back of this book I have included for you a number of prayers, a potpourri of sorts that is intended to be very relevant. You will find that most of the prayers included originate from either *A Course in Miracles* or from Gary Renard's insightful books. Some of these prayers I have also made up, added, or amended myself, for I find them invaluable in my search for some peace of mind. I am sure that Gary would not mind your using them, so you are free to use them any which way you please. There is at the back of the book a glossary of terms for those who are not so acquainted with the advanced and innovative material that is contained in this book.

Gentle reader, I dare not ask of you to believe in anything that I have written. I have completed this task from a hopefully inspired heart and used my powers of observation to the very best of my knowledge. As such, you should find the contents at least thought-provoking. I only want you to consider most carefully that which I have managed to compile here with an open mind, then let your Guide, the Holy Spirit, do the rest. After all, might He be trying to call you Home, too, and if so would you recognize it if He was? No one can resist God's Clarion forever, not you, not me.

No one!

Raymond Pratt
Lunasa 2006

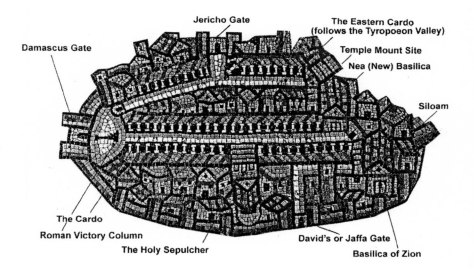

Jericho Gate

The Eastern Cardo
(follows the Tyropoeon Valley)

Damascus Gate

Temple Mount Site

Nea (New) Basilica

Siloam

The Cardo

Roman Victory Column

The Holy Sepulcher

David's or Jaffa Gate

Basilica of Zion

BYZANTINE JERUSALEM AROUND 560 C.E.

Chapter 1
If not God, Then Who?

*O*ne of the most profound effects on yours truly, as a very young lad, was my becoming an altar boy at the Jesuit Sacred Heart church on O'Connell Street, in the small Irish city of Limerick.

I grew up at a time when it was considered almost obligatory for every Irish mother to give up at least one of her sons to the Catholic Church. And many mothers had their own personal reasons and agendas regarding this, notwithstanding mine.

Missionary work was looked upon with awe by the local populace for it entailed a kind of white martyrdom. In the old Irish Celtic church between the sixth and ninth centuries, white martyrdom was the name given to the missionary's lot committed to spending most, if not all of their lives in foreign places spreading the Word of God to all. This would originate during the tumultuous centuries after the total fall of the western portion of the Roman Empire. In the fifth century C.E., the Vandals, with the Ostrogothic and Visigothic invaders to briefly name a few, would temporarily paralyze any advances in many areas of civilization brought about by the Roman Empire. Meanwhile, the eastern Byzantine section of the Roman Empire would remain intact until its own fall in the fifteenth century by Suleiman, whose fame you will hear of, a little later.

This was an enormous setback in learning and was indeed the beginning of the Dark Ages. This was also an age where Irish Celtic monks were very frequently called upon and who were willing enough to answer this far-off appeal for help. In this way, they would spread their own profound love of learning and spiritual luminescence to the disheartened masses of the darkening continent.

So after being accepted by the Jesuits (or the SJs as we fondly called them) into the old city of Limerick's Crescent College for their superior education at the ripe old age of seven, it was a natural progression to become an altar boy at the adjacent Jesuit church. The initiating process into this entirely new mental world for me would culminate in an extraordinary pride, taken-for-granted privilege, and a sense of belonging to a kind of spiritual Marine Corps. This whole aura of responsibility, status, tradition, pomp, and ceremony would have a profound and lasting effect on one of such tender years. However, I should sincerely like to have thought that this whole integrated learning experience a pleasing one. I would not like to have seen it manifest itself in some kind of trite sanctimoniousness and petty one-upmanship on my part!

My first memories of Crescent would be punctuated by some singular experiences of a relatively rare kind. Of such, I remember the arrival of Kenneth Kaunda, the very first president of the newly formed African state of Zambia, formerly Northern Rhodesia. He gave a speech I would never remember after a big roof-raising welcome from us. President Kenneth must have been educated by the Jesuit missionaries for I do remember he had some positive and productive things to say about them. But the thing that intrigued us mostly about Kenneth was his dark skin. This interest was probably whetted by the very obvious fact that any African leaders coming to Ireland in 1961 would be a once off event. This was the time when Britain was freeing her colonies in Africa. The thought of visiting our fair, green, and homogenous Irish republic would be as rare as hobbyhorses' teeth and sunny days in our own mid-Kerry county.

Prior to all this, the Salesian nuns, in my previous school at the Ferrybank convent, used to go on all the time about bringing "a penny for the black babies." This led, in the long run, to a collection box being put in each and every classroom, cast with the unfamiliar shape of a black African child's head. Below this small enigmatic head was a black metallic hand. When we placed one of our copper pennies thereon and depressed a lever, it would then rise up and the penny would disappear, in an instant, into its wide, gaping mouth. For all of us, this was such a scarily awesome and astounding sight! God forgive me for such innocence, but it was honestly like having your very own classroom cannibal! Such were the peculiar results of our young active minds from the thrilling stories brought back and told to us by the Irish missionary workers in Africa.

We did much of our learning by rote, which, it would seem, was the norm in the sixties. The lessons brought home included poetry, tables, catechism, Gaelic, of course, and even the altar boys' replies to the priests' rendition of the Latin Tridentine Mass. All of these were well learned and applied most eagerly. However, my knowledge of Latin would make my later study of Spanish and French a relatively easy task.

The one good thing about rote is that you are not inclined to forget anything that you have learned. And I still have the memories of past reminders in the form of corporal punishment to prove it. Here below, I have incorporated the first eight lines of the introduction to the Tridentine Mass in Latin and English.

Intribo ad Altari Dei, ad Deum qui laetificat
Iuventutem meum.
Adiorum nostrum Nomine Domini,
Qui faecit Coelum et Terram.

I will go to the Altar of God,
To God who rekindles my youth.
Let us adore the Name of God,
Who made Heaven and Earth.

It is within those very last two lines, "Qui faecit Coelum et Terram," that we bring you to the meat and bones of this chapter, for within it lies the unfamiliar "Fallacy of Ages." The last line is a typical comment on a primarily basic UNTRUTH, that being that God created the earth.

God did NOT make the earth!

Nor did he make the heavens above, as we know them. He did not make the idyllic seas or tempestuous tsunamis. Nor did He endeavor to make for us any special island paradises, nor sun-blasted deserts, all of which are the results of duality in action.

Utter blasphemy, I can hear a raucous cry go up, to arms! To arms now! Bring us back Torquemada and the Holy Inquisition!

It is not too difficult to effect, on some occasions, bold, original, and eccentric statements, but shooting from the hip is all too common for a writer. What one needs is something fairly solid and substantial to back such novel statements up with.

Yes, God is our Loving Creator and He has a Home there for us that has existed and still continues to exist from the time He created us. Why would God see a need to create another parallel world, unless He thought our real Home with Him in His World was not good enough for us? As for all this, it can only be the thoughts of a lunatic. It cannot make any sense at all, because what we consider perfect enough for the Father to exist in simply has to be good enough for us!

And then why would God endeavor to create such a faulty dualistic anomaly constrained by the limits of time and space? Is not the original Home the perfect place for His children? What is it about this earth that makes it a better place than the Father's abode? This can hardly be a correct assumption.

God, being all Spirit in essence, could hardly now be expected to create for His children something that almost perfectly resembles a very large prison (or some might say, a madhouse). Would He condemn His Loved Creations to an existence of toil, fear, and anxiety and to strive, pine, and die in their earthly sleep? Would He then subject them to all this and to be subjected to and bombarded with the insane notions of war, dogma, patriotism, religious intolerance, fear, and sickness? What about all the depravities that they ultimately bring? Were all these His Creations, too?

Tell me, Does that sound like a loving father?

Does that sound like Our Loving Father?Maybe it is time to think otherwise:

"Miracles fall like drops of healing rain from Heaven on a dry and dusty world, where starved and thirsty creatures come to die."

Hardly the description we would expect of a world made by our Father, the Creator, for his extensions of Love. And this last paragraph mentioned is taken from the book *A Course in Miracles*.

God did not create a world for us to be starved, thirsty, and dust-choked only to ultimately die!

So if not God, then who?Let us cast our memory back a little to the time when Yeshua was tempted in the Judean desert during His forty days of solitude, after He was baptized. The Adversary came to him in His weakened physical state and tempted Him three times. The first and second temptations we know about and pertain to displays of power. The third temptation was that if Yeshua would bow down to him and accept him as his overlord, he would receive all the lands, cities, and kingdoms of the world that he was showing Him. But Yeshua had already seen His adversary's grand design from afar and could recognize illusion when He saw it.

So how could the Adversary, or let's say the Devil if you wish, how could he offer something to Yeshua, that which was NOT considered of his creation? This world that we live in, was it not supposed to have been created by God? The simple answer to this implausible question is that it WAS indeed ego's to offer!

Yes, the Adversary, the Devil, Ego, they indeed are all different names for the same Master Illusionist who are one and the same. And they have this agenda that calls to keep us chained forever on this place we call earth. And if you honestly think that death itself brings some relief, think again, for our consciousness does not die, and remember we still have to clear that nasty gunk that prevails in the dark part of our consciousness. Ergo, another possible attempt at a fruitless life subject to the all-pervasive, incessant whims and totally empty promises of the Great Deceiver.

In the Tarot card pack, amongst the major arcana of twenty-one cards, is the number fifteen card, "The Devil." On this card there is a picture of the Devil, who has two naked humans held in chains. The card does not in any way symbolize the dark terrors of demonic possession but symbolizes our enslavement to rampant materialism by our own personal choice. On closer observation one notices that the chains around the necks of the humans are quite loose and relatively easy to slip off.

For so it is with the Adversary. If we are in chains then we have given our power to the Master of Illusion who holds hegemony over us as long as we want him to do so. Yeshua saw this illusion of being chained to this material world for what it was, and was able, at a very early stage, to overcome these pernicious but pathetic advances of ego.

So, essentially, ego did create this world, but not without more than a little help from ourselves. For we gave ego certain abilities, at its behest, in successfully hiding us supposedly from the "Wrath" of the Creator that we wrongly perceived, a decision to be regretted by us, the frightened and confused children of God.

Because of this decision we, in a sense, made an aspect of ourselves that was a counterpart to our Reality and our place in Heaven, giving it overlordship in this newly formed domain of duality. Ego, now with this new power obtained and firmly in its possession, was not in any way going to relinquish it, and this is how it plans to keep the status quo indefinitely. In all honesty, ego really is a creation of our own through the mismanagement of our split mind. Naturally, because it does not involve the creative abilities of our Father, which is very fortunate for us, it is ultimately doomed to extinction. We would not want our miscreations to be real now, would we? For if that were to be the case then we would be making the illusions real and we would then be truly lost. Like every single thing that we haphazardly miscreate, they must all be similarly flawed, for they do not and cannot have the Creator's imprimatur.

In Gary Renard's wonderfully comprehensive book, *The Disappearance of the Universe*, on page 81, Gary is discussing some of the St. Thomas sayings, namely logion 13. Yeshua had taken His Apostle Thomas aside to discuss some probable theological matters. This would arouse some interest with the other Apostles, who naturally asked what Yeshua had said personally to him. Thomas answered that if he told them what he had been told, they would pick up the rocks close by and stone him. Obviously the others were at that time not ready to accept something from Yeshua that might be misunderstood or at least misconstrued as blasphemy. However, the ascended masters that were appearing occasionally to Gary to urge him forward with his book and to promote his enlightenment did tell him what the three hidden sayings were;

"You dream of a desert, where mirages are your rulers and

tormenters, yet these images come from you."

"Father did not make the desert and your home is still with Him."

"To return, forgive your brother, for only then do you forgive yourself."

The world is not a real place. Just take a look inside an atom and see that most of it consists of empty space. The protons, neutrons, and electrons, they all take up an infinitesimally small area of the whole atom. Yet what we see in its physical form is something that we consider very real, albeit almost completely made out of nothing. The same is true of the whole universe, galaxies and star formations spinning and cart-wheeling in a whole lot of nothing! Ego wants us to believe in the "sanctity" of the fact that we are stardust material, children of the universe. It wants us to find our "true god" amongst the nebulae and astronomical wonders to give all of these "creations" some sense of spiritual legitimacy, a distinct patina of awe, sanctity, and holiness. But what a lie that all is!

The outer regions of space were simply created to divert and hide us from our own Inner Space, namely our own True Self. That's why it looks complicated and unending.

It is meant to seem that way!

Ego rules through division and subdivision, tricks and sleight-of-hand. It wants us to believe that all these so-called wonders that were created on this worldly level are holy. All it wants is us to see a parallel version of a "heaven" with itself as our very own special ersatz and counterfeit god.

Heaven on earth? God forbid! Leave the Illusionist and its illusions to the misled dreamers who are not yet quite ready to wake up to the Call Home!

Raymond Pratt
Iuil 2006

Chapter 2
Forgiving Ongoing Attacks

Attack and ego are synonymous. Personal attacks are always the ego at work where it does decidedly pay to remember that it gains all of its strength through guilt, separation, division, and the use of scarcity. This, then, must highlight a necessity for vigilance on everyone's behalf. Consider that we do not overcome ego and its exertions by attacking it, for that's what it wants you to do. No! A student of God sees only two real principles at work on his or her way homeward bound, and they are Love and Light. Where there is an attack perceived by us, there is a scarcity of Love and Light, which creates a profound need for it. So we counter all attacks with what is lacking, and this is when we begin to use the facilities of our higher Mind, the abode of the Holy Spirit. Know for certain that all attacks are, in essence, simply base perceptions; an illusion within an illusion. This we have to be aware of and it is why there's always a need to be constantly on guard against what is real and what is perceived.

The Holy Spirit teaches us clearly and correctly how to apply *A Course in Miracles* to all our brothers and sisters who are in error. Judging is not for us to avail of, because judging makes the illusion real, and how can we then ignore what is real in our space? It becomes a festering aggravation and another speed bump on our journey Home. So what we must do is forgive the illusion of attack, and by our forgiving our brothers and sisters in error we are forgiving ourselves, something we need to do as, are we not part of the illusion?

Of course we are!

That's why we are here in the first place; we created this illusion and all its related derivatives to "hide" from our Creator. Simply being aware of this perception is indeed a very large step in initiating our journey home, the journey that began and will surely end in the same place it started; just like the prodigal son's return.

God, our Father, does not know forgiveness, for to know forgiveness is to imply guilt by His Own creation, namely His Own children. Who can be guilty who's a creation of the Hands of God? Our Father does not and cannot countenance for a moment what humans take mistakenly as guilt and justice for He sees it simply as human frailty. Guilt and fear are flaws created by man, and guilt cannot exist in the non-dual world of God's infinite and all-encompassing Love. So if we live in this world's projected illusion, at any given moment in time, it's only of a temporary measure. We have then decided to make it real by our judgmental behavior and non-forgiveness, which, by their design, really do not exist themselves! Even this whole idea of forgiveness in itself is not real, but it exists for us as a positive and exquisite perception that puts us back on the right track. So if all is just perception, nothing bad has really occurred and we are INNOCENT; however, this will not serve as a white card to orchestrate whatever we wish, as a lack of concern for our brother or sister can keep us reincarnating. Not all future incarnations are scripted to be comfortable and will, no doubt, include perceived harsher lessons in true forgiveness if not acted upon now. Consciousness does not die with the body, but it returns again to a new life with all its tiresome foibles and previous idiosyncrasies. This is most necessary as error still exists in the subconscious, an area where error needs to be expunged. We cannot go home without our brother or sister because the nature of our spiritual home does not exist in the "was" or "will be," It exists in the "now." That is what Yeshua meant when he instructed His disciples with the following statement, which can be interpreted at least three different ways. The third statement is the one I find most enlightening:

"The Kingdom of God is at hand,"
"The Kingdom of God is amongst you,"

and my favorite,

"The Kingdom of God is within you."

Yeshua was using the present tense here, just like His Father used with Moses on Mount Sinai, when He was talking to his disciples.

A Course in Miracles has this to say:

"Time and Eternity cannot both be real, because they contradict each other. If you will accept only what is timeless as real, you will begin to understand eternity and make it yours."

What's eternal does not need a timeline as eternity is now, the present, with no delays being necessary due to some future perceived existence. And although it may seem that we all go Home to the Father separately and at different times, we all go home together, for it cannot be any other way!

Our innocence is one of the first views of what's behind one of the veils, the same veils we put up with the smoke and mirrors to hide us from the illusory "Wrath of God."

Consider Adam hiding fearfully from the Father who "made" him, after he had eaten of the Tree of Knowledge. We have this fear of God woven into the many veils that we use to hide from Him, our Perfect Parent.

This unwarranted deception was a deal done long ago with ego, who cultivated in us an unnatural fear of our existence outside the Godhead, creating a base lie regarding the nature of our own Father. The fact is that this whole immeasurable universe was created to hide from God. A world so beautiful and yet oh! so false, but ego's way to show us its version of holiness on the altar of form, a fallacy and contradiction from beginning to end, from the temporal lord of time and space, ego. God does not and cannot hate, for discord and special favors are the sole creations of the realm of ego. God simply has no room in Heaven for anything else but Love and Light of which we are an integral part.

Remember, forgiveness has to be the only key. The Holy Spirit promises a miracle each and every time we use the advanced forgiveness process. If we are indeed truly worried about how many times we should consider forgiving our trespassers, did He, Yeshua, not say to us "seven times seventy"? In other words He implied that we should NEVER, EVER stop forgiving, for it makes our perceived journey home that much shorter.

I have been led to believe for certain that correct advanced forgiveness, when surrendered and released to the Holy Spirit, will bring about almost instantaneous results. We have nothing to lose by trying and a whole lot more to gain, because any door ajar to the Holy Spirit is a door wide open to His Munificence. He forgives that which we cannot reach in our subconscious, while we need to forgive those who need to be forgiven in our lives. We also need to forgive those who have gone on before us in death, unforgiven.

When we made that "fatal" mistake (as ego would have us believe) where the idea of "What if?" placed us in a desperate position where we could exist outside God's domain, albeit confused, fearful, and guilt-ridden, the Holy Spirit was created. He, acting as an extension of God the Father, was to extend Himself like a life raft, and be the all-embracing, intimate, and eternal Rescuer by His Pure Love in action. There was never, ever any possibility of our being carried away or drowning in the maelstroms that ego continues to provide for us. And just like some divine hologram, the Holy Spirit carries the complete healing abilities of the Creator; nothing is restricted nor in any way diminished. The Holy Spirit is an extension of this Love, and we know why He exists; he exists because He is a part of us and we are a part of Him. All He wants us to do is to end for good this whole perceived separation that we continue to entertain.He wants us Home!

Raymond Pratt
Marta 2006.

Chapter 3
The Devil You Know & Don't Know

*B*efore time as we know it began, and long before man found himself in this unsatisfactory place that he mistakenly called home, a battle raged in the Heavens between God the Father and another powerful entity by the name of Lucifer.

This potent "Prince of Light," to be known chiefly as Lucifer (Latin: from lux, light; lucifer, meaning light-bringer) was God's supposed chosen one, and would epitomize in every sense all of what we might regard a kingdom's general-in-command to be. He was haughty, arrogant, all-powerful, handsome, and just a shade too ambitious for his own good. On his long epic journey downward toward the Pit, what would have been his most intimate thoughts? What kind of opinion would he have had of his newly created domain? Would he have had the focused composure to say to himself:

"The mind can make a hell out of heaven and a heaven out of hell."

And still could he believe it? Regardless, the mind would have to have made a fairly large abode for his accompanying legions, at most, a very substantial number indeed!

Is this a plausible story? Well, hardly!

Lucifer's "fall from heaven" is common knowledge to a majority of the more significant Christian belief systems where he is known as the Prince of Darkness, the Adversary, and the Great Deceiver. Other lesser-known denominations will personify him to such a ludicrous extent, with the results ranging from almost comical to corny. All of this, however, does honestly smack a little too much of theatrics. And then again, isn't it true that man has always been good at playing parts so much that he has, on occasion, needed to be reminded of who he really is.

So what have the theatrics of man got to do with this story, and as for Lucifer, who was he really and what role does ego play in all this, as surely it does? Was man now playing, by choice, a supporting or leading role? I would like to interrupt the story just a little bit by vaguely similar ideas that now can be gleaned from a relatively new book called *A Course in Miracles*. How about our "fall from grace" or how "Paradise was lost" by man's own misdirection and decisions, and by his need for an "ally" during a time of "Great Confusion"?

Similarities are one thing; coincidences are another question for which I do not hold to the general idea that they are elements of chance! What is put before us then should be correctly acted upon in a timely manner. All coincidences are generally learning opportunities that, on a very regular basis, need to repeat themselves if missed the first time around.

That's why they are coincidental!

There was a time when man also dwelt within the embrace of God's domain, a perfect and guilt-free image of the Creating Father, holding love and free agency in an inviolate existence. Man would, by birthright, share the heavens with his Creator during an indistinct blip in eternity, a mental hiccough in Heaven; he then decided to take time out, and a little space, to travel a dead-end spur line. How he did this was by acting on the very fleeting notion but erroneous idea that there might be something outside the Oneness of the Father that he might be in need of knowing about.

This was a kind of illusion or dreamtime for man, not real, but it would seem to create the perception of an anomaly in the Oneness of heaven, a kind of polyp protruding through the fabric of eternity. Man would always be still connected to this eternal realm, but he would be almost completely surrounded by the utter chaos of a split and dualistic mind. This split mind could only be set against itself and subject to, when deluded on a fairly regular basis, the insane thought system that would now mostly envelop it from there on. So Man from here would, unfortunately, be dreaming in exile.

But it is reasonable for us to assume that in the dominions of the Infinite Reality, all suppositions and notions can be scripted, acted out, and allowed by an understanding and doting Father who knows the divine and exquisite nature of our eternal being. This decision by itself would eventually place man within the present existence that he finds himself today.

So, in effect, this point in time during what I call the "Great Confusion" is where there was an instant when we genuinely thought that we could entertain the idea of an existence outside and independent of God's domain. We then mistakenly made a bargain with another aspect of our mind that would begin to exist autonomously. How this occurred was that we went from the simple clarity of Oneness to the daunting interplay of twoness, or if you really wish, duality in action. This could only create for us a most perplexing dilemma, for we were used to the eternal Love and Light of the Oneness and we were now faced with the miscreation of a dark hole, an opposite. The opposite of light was, for us, indeed dark or absence, and the opposite of love was, nooooo! it was not hate, the obvious choice. It was fear.

Thus, fear, now acting as the bane of man, from here onward would rule man's lower mind. It would always be instrumental in the need to project what we don't like about ourselves on our fellow brother. Or see a need to project the same dislike outwards and again miscreate, yes, a drum-roll please, yours truly, the Devil.

Both our unfortunate brother and the devil could be now considered scapegoats and perfectly valid culprits in initiating the profound lack of love so very noticeable in our world of today. That is, of course, if we hadn't in the meantime found another legitimate target, for the ego at least, in attacking our very own selves!

We must remember that at all times, love and forgiveness are the two main items so very necessary for our return journey. Without them, our return home is temporarily blocked because anytime there is any kind of lack perceived, there is always a need. It is a need that can only be directed toward fulfillment, not by receiving, but by the selfless giving of oneself freely, totally, and unconditionally.

The thing to remember is that all this was perceived at a different level. We were really dreaming this incident and there was never any sustained threat to our eternal reality, although this very new element of fear that we deemed to create would most certainly want us to think so. But dreams can and will be, even for the hardiest, nightmares that feel at any given time real enough. The answer to them lies with help from our Teacher, the One who can only teach Truth, the Holy Spirit Himself, and we can then commence the waking up process, but again this can only happen if we really want it to.

So how did we come to the idea of a personified and malevolent Devil? Most of our spiritual evolvement comes from the notion of monotheism, a belief in one single God that probably started with the Hebrew God, during the days of Abraham and Sarah. Many of the tribes of Canaan had separate belief systems in direct competition with the Israelites, who, themselves, were unique in their belief in the one God. That God would have the unpronounceable Name of YHVH (YAHWEH) so that it could never, ever be used in any blasphemous manner by Israel's enemies.

The enemies of Israel, namely the ever present and nearby Philistines, the Amalekites, and Edomites to name but a few, had their own gods, Moloch, Dagon, Baal, and so on. Moloch followers sacrificed their firstborn to their chief idol, and this was seen as simply monstrous by the Israelites. But did not the patriarch Abraham almost do the same thing to his firstborn son as well when it was asked of him?

The name "Bel" or "Baal" is very common throughout the ancient world. It means lord and can even be found in the Celtic divinities. A good example would be the Irish Gaelic where the month of May is called "Bealtaine," "Baal" meaning lord and "Tine" meaning fires, hence "Lord of the Fires." Mhi Bealtaine (i.e. the month of May) started on the evening of the thirtieth of April, six months exactly before and after the Halloween or Samhain festival. The Celtic day, it should be noted too, started on the evening prior, something it shared with the Jewish commencement of the twenty-four-hour day.

"Baal" turns up also in the New Testament where a number of the people, while witnessing His great works, wanted to charge Yeshua for performing miracles in the name of Belzebub or Belzebul. Both words are related to quite different things. Belzebub or Baal Zebub meant "Lord of the Flies." The other word mentioned, Belzebul, or Baal Zebul, was used in a depreciating and scornful way, especially for non-believers and heretics; it meant "Lord of Dung." The connotation here was to imply that Yeshua was close to being, if He was not already, an apostate and not worthy of being listened to.

It should be noted, too, that our notion of Hell also stems from this very same region, and specifically the old city of Jerusalem. This city nearly always had a fairly large population that increased quite substantially during Pessach or Passover. (The exception naturally was during the time of the Exodus, the Captivity in Babylon and the Diaspora.) This would have to be considered as the most sacred and holy place to give thanks to the Jewish God, YHVH (YAHWEH) or Elohim because of its huge temple being the center of the ancient Jewish sacrificial belief system.

THE VALLEYS OF JERUSALEM IN 30 C.E.

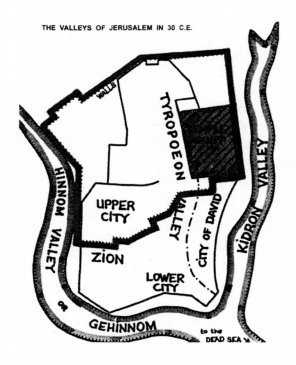

To the southwest of the city lay the deep Hinnom Valley where the city's trash was taken and burnt. As you can imagine there was very probably a dark and constant pall of smoke, with a foul and fetid stench emanating from here at any given time, a place you would not normally wish to be seen in. And so what is it that we have, when a large collection of trash and debris appears? Flies, and a whole lot of them.

And there we have it, all in one place, a burning dump crawling with flies, Beelzebub's own minions and domain. The Hebrew word for Hell is Gehinnom and it derives from the proper noun "Hinnom," the name of the valley that we have taken into consideration. So if our plan is to find the original Hell, we should endeavor to start looking for it somewhere in that valley situated to the southwest of the Sha'ar Yafah, the Jaffa Gate of the old city. A good view of its original setting can be seen from the fifteenth century walls, which Suleiman the Great, the Turkish sultan, rebuilt, and where the Migdal Daveed, the Tower of David, is also located.

We have the innate ability to create many things both good and bad as can be expected in this world of duality. As for Hell, the world we co-created can most certainly be that, if we wish it so. As for the Devil, what we don't like about ourselves we are inclined to project somewhere else. Remember the word Lucifer means "light-bringer," which really is what all creations of the Father are. Again, this harks back to the idea that ego is the creation of a light-bringer, another faulty creation of the children of God, for it simply could not exist, having duality within the eternal Home. It could have only been created by a previous denizen of heaven, another light-bringer, namely we ourselves. Fortunately for us, all of our creations are subject to a very temporary existence, so ego's reign can only be at best and in the long run, limited.

In the book *A Course in Miracles*, the chapter regarding the "Condition of Reality" on page 210, it is shown that the ego may see some good in humanity, but if this is so, it is only for its own special purposes, which would most certainly NOT include the paving of the way to your own ultimate resurrection of the mind and subsequent return to the Father:

"The ego may see some good, but never only good. That is why its perceptions are so variable. It does not reject goodness entirely, for that you could not accept. But it always adds something that is not real to the real, thus confusing illusion and reality. For perceptions cannot be partly true. If you believe in truth and illusion, you cannot tell which is true."

And also:

"You have made many ideas that you have placed between yourself and your Creator, and these beliefs are the world as you perceive it. Truth is not absent here, but it is obscure."

The creation of ego seems to suit us perfectly (after all, why not? Did we not create it?) for we have forgotten what lies behind the veils, those same veils created by ourselves alone simply to hide us from the One God, our Parent. By giving ego credence, our unfailing gullibility and by letting ourselves submit to its agenda we end up also projecting all the fears that we have constantly dreamt up. Those incessant fears, of which there are so many, also include the fear of God, the fear of Heaven, blame, guilt, or whatever, on anything that will not remind us of our own True and Loving Nature. Another excerpt from the *Course* shows us what ego has in store for all of us:

"Remember, then, that whenever you look without and react unfavorably to what you see, you have judged yourself unworthy and have condemned yourself to 'death.' The death penalty is ego's ultimate goal, for it fully believes that you are a criminal, as deserving of death as God knows you are deserving of life. The death penalty never leaves the ego's mind for that is what it always reserves for you in the end. Wanting to kill you as the final expression of its feeling for you, it lets you live but to await death. It will torment you while you live, but its hatred is not satisfied until you die. For your destruction is the one end toward which it works, and the only end with which it will be satisfied."

How can we let such a thing happen? Was it by sheer complacency or a general lack of vigilance? For is this not some kind of spiritual sleeping tablet, a potion that was provided to us unwittingly, with the dubious compliments of our own insane dreamtime doctor, ego itself?

A second opinion is definitely called for, and He is always quiet, attentive, and very close by!

Raymond Pratt
Lunasa 2006

Chapter 4
The Inconsistency of "Rapture"

Many fundamentalist and evangelical Protestants, even in our present day and age, believe in a peculiarity called "The Rapture." This stems from the nineteenth century period, at a time when a young United States was evolving and expanding rapidly across the great North American continent. With the expansion came new and sometimes spurious versions of God's Word in its wake. It left these fallow and newly opened lands, readily available and at the hands of the many various, often intrusive and occasionally unscrupulous religious "crusaders" of the day. Many of these single-minded men epitomized the current idea of the time, that of the unbridled growth and idyllic "Manifest Destiny" syndrome inherent in the United States expansion.

During this time the various denominations were quite numerous and they included the vanguard of the new protestant reform movement, the Latter-day Saints (i.e. the Mormons), Jehovah's Witnesses, and a number of others. Catholicism had, for the most part, other necessities to deal with as the notion of professing this faith intimated allegiance to a foreign power, namely Rome and the Papal States. Because of this intimation, intolerance was unquestionably rife against Poles, Irish, and the Germans. It was particularly prevalent in the fledgling US Army, a white racist-ridden protestant and Anglo-Saxon bastion.

The Rapture entails Christ returning to earth at the end of days or some predetermined time. This end of days is supposedly preceded by an era of tribulation where many suffer prior, during, or after the removal of "God's Chosen." It does not matter whether you believe in the pre-tribulation, mid-tribulation, or post-tribulation Rapture; all of them entail the complete disappearance of a significant portion of the believing population.

The idea that a certain portion of believers end up disappearing leads me to consider that ego is at play here as there is the "Special Relationship" involved. In *A Course of Miracles*, special relationships are a sign of division and guilt, where the division then suggests a hierarchy of souls, and the guilt, in this case, is laid at the feet of the ones who have not disappeared. This then creates a supposed deficiency and implies that the "non-desparisados," i.e. the non-disappeared, are unprepared, unaware, or simply ineligible for God's plan.

Can God be benign and selective in one action?

Can God leave part of his flock to the potential wolf? Hardly!

Could ego do this? Absolutely. The lord of division and scarcity has his own "eternal" plan that does call to keep us in error to the end of days. This is ego's way of rule, the rule of dualistic thinking; if there's white, there's got to be black. If there's light, there's got to be darkness. God's Way always was totally different. God sees Love where there is Light, and God sees a need for love where there's no Light. The significant difference being that nothing of any importance exists except Love and Light, and to Him, nothing else matters!

The Holy Spirit, or literally the Breath of God, the Ruach Ha-Kodesh is man's connection with the Holy Trinity. When we existed in the Light, we made some incorrect considerations that led us to be temporarily here, He was, is, and always will be the bright shining beacon leading us home. Just like the fiery pillar at night and the rising pillar of smoke during the day that led the Israelites home across the Sinai desert to their beloved Canaan.

Remember Yeshua's Parable of the Lost Sheep where He tells us that one lost soul is more important than the ninety-nine saved? God wants all of us back home, and what son's father wouldn't want this? God simply could not exist if there was indeed any element of selectivity in His all-embracing Love; consequently we could not exist. The fact that we do is proof positive that we are the product of His never ending Love, and what's of God goes back to God, regardless. The only question is a matter of when, a decision NOT made by God but by ourselves.

But it would be incorrect to imply in this case that our sisters and brothers are wrong with regard to the idea of "The Rapture." It must be remembered that it is a relatively new concept that has existed only for about a hundred and seventy years. It is a peculiarity of these United States and not a common belief in the rest of the Christian world. It must be remembered also that some element of truth does exist in nearly all belief systems to a point. What must be done by us is to glean and save what pertains to the truth here and release that which we have no need of to the Holy Spirit. Our lower minds are always suspect to finding fault and effectively projecting guilt on our brothers, so all possible error must be forgiven, then surrendered and released immediately to the Holy Spirit. Any attempt to correct it ourselves alone would imply a judgment call against our brother. This is something we are not going to do on one whose sole reason to exist is in holding the key to our own salvation. No judgments, not now, not ever!

Raymond Pratt
Samhain 2005

Chapter 5
Mindfulness and Judicial Execution

*I*t is true that all of us perceive ourselves at various stages of spiritual evolution, although evolution is probably not the best choice of words here, as it might imply the idea of status. We are souls progressing down the same divine path that ultimately, we believe, leads back to our unique origins, that being of the Godhead, the Creator, and the Jewish Elohim/Shekinah of old.

Our path generally is by no means easy, but one we chose ourselves from a number of possibilities scripted in our pre-existence. Some of those are choices within choices that may well indeed involve perceived life-and-death situations. Whether those choices are to be made on the operating table, in the courtroom, or on some battlefield, or even on death row, they are still multiple answer choices that will have a perceived profound effect on the speed of our soul's return journey home. Our only real choice in this world is to love and forgive and to abstain from any type of judgment call.

No choice can be completely wrong, nor for that matter can it be endorsed as wholeheartedly right in the world of time and space. What concerns us, however, is how one comes to one's conclusions. If we succumb to the emotions or defer to the mass media spectacles and public interest caravan, then our conclusions will have to be suspect. This is because all kinds of impressions originating from the mass consciousness are most certainly subject to its lower and dense vibrational common denominator, the locale of ego.

Many of us will try to use truths as a deciding factor in our decision-making process, but what is truth? Indeed Pontius Pilate was known to ask this intriguing question under similar circumstances.

Is my truth different from your truth? And if my truth differs from yours, is there a hierarchy of different truths where my truth holds more precedence over yours, because my values or my god differs from yours?

There's only one truth and that is if God is all-loving and eternal, where we ourselves are made in God's image with souls that are eternal, then the real truth is that we have an eternity to address and resolve our transgressions. And that includes even those who we perceive wrongly as the most sinful of us. After all, what is sin but an opportunity and a sincere chance for us to correct our aim; indeed the word in Hebrew means "to miss the mark."

With all this in mind, we should consider the death penalty for a moment. Our intrinsic need to balance the books, this most basic need for revenge, which stems from a time even before the Mosaic Law was laid down in the Old Testament, is highly prevalent in much of the United States. Execution is such an exceptionally brutal weapon for a first world country to try to engage in, and it is a solution lambasted by most of the western free world. However, any eye for an eye policy enforced simply makes everyone blind. Who here, in all honesty, could seriously venture in being God's smiting hand incarnate on Earth? Who here is ready and willing to cast the first stone? And who here is without "sin"?

When we deign to execute someone, it is not that we are terminating prematurely that person's sacred contract with God. What happens here on this sick planet is of no consequence to God, for He and He alone understands the true and everlasting nature and destiny of His Own Creations. But executions can and do create major conundrums with regards to those interlinked elements of remorse and repentance.

When we deem to have or even entertain this basic need to execute what is creating our fear, there is a lesson for us there to be learnt. The element of fear, all instigated by the perpetrator, it would seem, needs to be attacked so we then see a need to execute. The results as such, far from bringing any satisfaction, never, ever seem to ensure the smallest measure of lasting peace of mind to any of the victim's relatives and friends.

Remember, love does not destroy, and fear is the lack of love, so executions are not a valid choice for a student of God to indulge in. Remorse and repentance are a very necessary part of the forgiveness process, and an early date set for execution, or even the threat of one, is probably bound to instill a negative mind-set on the perpetrator's side. Repentance is most necessary. It means, in Greek, to stop doing what you are doing and "turn around," something that every single "lost soul" needs to embrace no matter what they've done.

A Course in Miracles is quite adamant about the need to forgive. It has this to say this about judgment calls:

> "Everything you behold without is a judgment of what you behold within. If it is your judgment it will be wrong, for judgment is not your function. If it is the judgment of the Holy Spirit it will be right, for judgment IS His function. You share His function only by judging as He does, reserving no judgment at all for yourself. You will judge against yourself, but He will judge for you."

The divine spark lives in each and every one of us, good, bad, and indifferent. It is the same spark that guides us all to our remaking, and all through the Holy Spirit for the final return Home. How can we become an integral part of God when we cannot learn to forgive? How can we exist as a loving extension of the Father when we cannot accept the true remorse and repentance of a brother or sister in error?

We must remember that "sin" is simply a cry for help to the Holy Spirit, for are not all souls innocent?

When we consider the so-called dregs of society, the poor, the sick, the flotsam and jetsam spewed up on life's uncaring shore, I am reminded of a story I read a couple of months ago about an old retired man who was walking on his local beach after a severe storm. Before him were literally thousands of starfish cast up on the beach. The old man carefully started to pick up and place some of the stranded starfish back in the surf. After a short while of doing this, a younger man casually approached the old man and declared incredulously,

"There must be thousands of starfish lying on the beach. You just can't put them all back in the sea, and what difference are you going to make anyway?"

The old man thought for a second and looked down at the starfish nestled in his two hands before caringly putting it back in the surf, and he quietly said,

"It makes a difference to this one."

Even our very smallest endeavors that involve our brothers become wayside markers that are noted and consequently are a part of a strategy that we scripted into our final journey Home. But let there be no doubt about it, for the truth is, that we ALL go Home eventually!

Raymond Pratt
Meitheamh 2005

Chapter 6
Theta Healing, Going Up to God

The month of May 2005, after starting out very well for me, was now beginning to change into a particularly problematic time. Cristin, my only daughter, and I had returned from a couple of days' R&R on the island of Oahu in the Hawaiian islands, a truly well-earned and enjoyable rest for both of us. Brendan, my nineteen-year-old son had once again failed to contact me about accompanying us, and I knew in my heart something was brewing within him. But little did I know that it would be quite some time before he would see or even speak to me again.

No sooner had I gotten into the general swing of things, when my Saab's computer went completely on the blink. This is something that you would not expect from a 1999 European car, but the 1,000-dollar-plus bill had to be duly paid.

Also Linda, my second oldest sister, in San Antonio, Texas, who had always had a generous heart regarding me, now needed a large sum of money to tide her over some unfortunate personal circumstances that arrived at her doorstep. Linda, funnily enough, would be the sister who would leave a rather strange blue book on my dining room table before she returned to Texas, as a little present for me.

This book would change my life so completely that I felt that my whole past life was spent marking time for this occasion. With all these distracting escapades going on, you could only assume that this might not be the most opportune time to begin learning the simplest basics of Theta Healing, but I had planned on it and wanted it, and I was simply raring to go!

Alice, my teacher, lives only a mile or two from where I live in Stansbury Park in Utah, by crow's flight. It is a quiet new neighborhood with tremendous views of the Oquirrh mountain range.

Alice is most fortunate, for she does own a quaint, very peaceful, and secluded wooden house in the high valleys where the Summit and Wasatch counties meet, about an hour's drive away. This house is conveniently located in Midway, a small and beautifully located Swiss village with honest-to-God real Swiss descendents.

It was during the evening of an early summer's day that I arrived in the village of Midway and we spent some of the last remaining hours informing ourselves about this awesome neighborhood and getting to know each other's acquaintance. The next day we were avid students learning how to put ourselves into Theta mode. This is where we change our brain rhythms from Alpha to Theta mode so that we can then try to observe certain phenomena and initiate healing. We were all asked to find a partner to work with and to then start a process of intense screening, a kind of medical bio-scanning lesson.

Terry, a very good friend of Alice's, happened to be my partner, and I began to initiate the Theta mode for the first time so that I could do a medical screening. For me, this was quite a novel exercise where one stands closely behind the prospective subject and then touches that person's shoulders. The students need to close their eyes and slowly mentally project out of and in front of them self, all to end up facing the subject. The results occasionally can be quite startling!

A short time later, the projected mental image of a body appeared before my own closed eyes. It looked a little gray, brown, and white, and it was almost like I was looking at an old x-ray film negative or a sepia-colored photograph. That was all very well and good, but as I continued to scan the lower abdomen area of Terry, I saw a large collection of little black dots that really looked like buckshot. This to me was fascinating and I found it rather amusing, but later when I had brought this to Terry's attention, she mentioned to me that she had been suffering from acute endometriosis. She could have been telling me that this was some type of neck whiplash, electrical shock, or parasite infection, for all of the accumulated knowledge of "endo" that I was aware of, and that was, well, in one word, nonexistent. But these results themselves were to be satisfactory enough for Alice, and it allowed me to proceed on to my next partner.

My very next subject was to be Bobbi, who can only be described as a very upbeat, friendly, and dedicated New Age teacher, and who has had some quite chronic medical problems. The quick results of my own personal medical screening on Bobbi were extraordinary enough for the acquired information it revealed. The lucidity as to what was made available to me was startling through the use of Theta sight, but this was not to be before scaring the absolute "bejasus" out of me.

I sat Bobbi down in a chair and started my Theta screening, and I found that a picture was fast becoming visible to me. I saw, in her chest cavity area, a noticeably large square form, unequally divided into white or bright and black or dark areas. The lighter area took up about three-quarters of this square, but the rest was very dark. It was here that I began to become aware of another new color, that being red. What I saw was particularly clear! I saw red bubbles or possibly platelets all originating and streaming from the light area toward the darker area and then disappearing. This naturally, seemed to me to be a very ominous portent. Was this a warning to be taken or an alert, for well you may have asked me then! I could not know!

I asked Bobbi if she had ever been diagnosed with a hole or murmur in her heart. She straightforwardly said to me that yes, she had a heart aneurism. This was all a little too much for me. I rushed down the flight of stairs, out into the front garden, and proceeded to wrap myself around the very closest and biggest old oak tree I came in contact with.

Bobbi would have a non-fatal heart attack five days later!

Laurie was my next subject, but now we were going to do a head and shoulders scanning to see what might lie there outside the medical field. This, in effect, was to be more of a paranormal scan.

Using the same sequences I had previously used, I took a stand behind Laurie; I saw above her head, after a very short while, the word "NETZACH" as plain as day. Over her right shoulder, the segment may very well have been empty, but over her left one was what I thought to be a rather wolf-like creature. When I tried hard to focus on the creature, it retreated out of my vision. Alice, my Theta teacher, thinking that it might be a "wayward" (or possibly a "familiar") sent it away toward the light. Incidentally, the word Netzach is one of the "Tree of Life's" spheres as in the Qabbalah and it does come from the Hebraic language for it stands for Victory. It is associated with the Archangels Hamiel and Uriel.

When asked to do another bio-scan for someone, I felt a little unworthy. That, of course, would have to be ego playing its nasty little guilt game that it incessantly tries to inflict on us on a very regular occasion. I cannot remember for certain the name of the person who asked this of me; I think it might have been Angela. However, I did reluctantly agree to do it.

In this case I scanned from the head downwards. As I passed by the right eye, the symbol of a telescopic sight appeared just below it. I continued my screening and a transparent square appeared over the lower back area. I asked for the area to be highlighted and the same square focused in greater detail on the lower coccyx.

A small black indefinite teardrop mass appeared to exist in the lower left abdominal area, but I just could not ascertain its exact location. Later I spoke to the subject and she advised me that she was having some sinus problems below her right eye and suffered from chronic back pain. I also had to advise her of the teardrop mass that I had seen and where it was generally located in the midriff area, and that an X-ray might be just the proper option to avail of.

A few months later in Long Island while attending Sonia's, my youngest sister's wedding ceremony, Marie, my oldest sister (whom I have always, ever since I was a young child, called Memer), asked me to perform one of my bio-scans. I reluctantly agreed again, for weddings do usually involve just a little alcohol, and I had had a few drinks with all of my extended family members who were here visiting from Britain and Ireland. Marie was adamant so I quickly relented as I would not be seeing her again for a while.

In Marie's case, a new color would appear for me and this time the contrast between light and dark grew quite strong. The new color that was visible was a very light electric blue-green, and this

I could see in the form of a see-through circular helmet grid surrounding the top of Marie's head. This, it would seem, was there to emphasize her major sinus problems. A strong, wide, tight band of the same earlier color could be seen also around her chest, and Marie tells me that she suffered from a major asthma attack just about six to twelve hours later. Two medium light brown areas also might have needed to be seen to, the right knee area and in the lower left breast area, which hopefully she would have had checked in due time.

At this time, my faith in the Holy Spirit was growing as I now had been introduced to *A Course in Miracles*, which was changing large areas of my perception. In the Theta healing process, we do command the Holy Spirit to help us with our special sight and healing, and I have to say that I was having a bit of a problem with that. I did not feel too comfortable about trying to command an aspect of God to do any of my bidding especially when I should have been surrendering and accepting Him as my own Guide. I decided to call, on one occasion, for the Holy Spirit's quiet help when I was about to give my very first class that would relate to the Course. I tried to talk to Him prior, as a class of thirty people was indeed substantial, but as I was entering the building I heard in what I can only call my mind's ear:

"You know I always help you."

No! I am not suffering from any spiritual delusions; I am a very very down-to-earth person. In fact you would have to be very hard-pressed indeed to find a more connected and well-grounded "double earth" Taurean, with a Virgo ascendant spirit in your local vicinity.

Nevertheless, after those initial classes with Alice, which I did find beneficial, I continued to teach but now with much more of *A Course in Miracles* slant in mind. I was beginning to find teaching the classes to be a very frustrating ordeal, as all our earlier progress, to me, seemed to have petered out. I really wanted to blame someone, perhaps even my own students, but the fault, if there was any, would have to have been mine alone, for I am more than just a trifle impatient. I did sense a strong need in me to get through to a larger audience. I did not see the need within that was more concerned at healing souls at the ego's lower "minds joined" level, which was the class's curriculum. However, before any of these changes could occur, I would later return to Alice's intermediate class in the mountains that fall to receive some more instruction and my Theta healing practice certificate.

The intermediate class was again commencing in its original setting in the Wasatch mountains for the following November. It was a little less entertaining, but the course had a great deal more information to offer. I guess I am to suppose that the novelty of Theta by this time had worn off a bit. Still, we had some of our very original subjects and I did get to repeat a bio-scan on Bobbi, something I was really looking forward to doing.

I should say that I found Alice always to be a wonderful teacher. She was patient and painstakingly thorough in her applications. I had never, in my studies, seen Alice show any signs of frustration with any of her students, and I do wish her well for I have a lot to thank her for.

After commencing this intermediate class, Bobbi came over to me and asked, not surprisingly for me, to do a new bio-scan. She had not forewarned me in any way of her ongoing predicament; however, she did look reasonably healthy. Bobbi is so charismatic in outlook that it is always hard to see if one is really seeing the suffering being, behind the smiles.

I sat Bobbi down and started the bio-scan, and lo and behold! What a fine sight to see! I saw a plethora of signs and symbols all over her. But the thing that stood out the most pertained most significantly to her heart condition. The original large black and white square had gone, and all I could see of it now were remnants of tiny light and dark fragments lazily heading away from her central body mass. This was of course in the same place where the two-tone square was seen. Where her heart would have been was a goblet, a grail, or I should say, a chalice, one very similar to the chalice one sees in the Tarot deck. It greatly resembled the minor arcana card, i.e. the Ace of Cups. Issuing forth from the chalice was a fountain, like some hidden fountain of eternal youth, or maybe there were connotations that might also suggest some notions of the Holy Grail. The explanations could go on and on.

Anyhow, they were only symbols, just like words are, and to me they symbolized a new lease on life for Bobbi.

I noticed that her left kidney looked very pale and inflamed, if that's the right word. Bobbi then told me that she suffers from pernicious anemia. So much has to be said for Theta sight.

Incidentally I also saw a very large gray owl with its wings splayed, as for protection, above her head. The owl is an old symbol for occult knowledge, and being a night-bird, it does have close associations with the night goddess Lillith, who is ruler of the dark side of the Moon. Luna, the Moon, rules over what you see at night. Lillith rules over what you DON'T see at night. In some circles Lillith has been considered by some beliefs as Adam's first wife that is before Eve ever came along.

Jeri, one of my astrologer acquaintances, asked me for a scan of her head and shoulders area. Behind her I could see a large oyster shell pulsating purple light. On her right side segment, I saw a dark fish, but on her left side was a little display that I would be hard-pressed to explain or elaborate on. However Jeri may be able to see some sense in it.

Terri, if you will remember from the previous class, was there and she wanted a future reading, so I tried to do this in Theta. This was totally new for me; I saw it as a challenge and accepted it willingly. The results were quite colorful, very descriptive, and full of symbology.

I began to see tall, slick, evergreen trees with a small dark cabin half hidden in them. Beside this view lay the old bones of a medium-sized fish. Now we were having a distinct picture of a wet coastal evergreen area. Then I saw two pneumatic wheels set in an axle and the deep unmistakable imprint of a bear paw beside it. It was now getting easier to come up with explanations. In all this symbology, I foretold a trip to either Washington, Alaska, B.C. in Canada or Oregon. Terri had told me that she and her husband had been recently planning to travel northwest to Bellingham or Whidbey Island within a year or so. I knew that both the city and island were located in the state of Washington. Now whether I was picking up on their interest of simply traveling there or whether this planned journey in itself would be a fait accompli in the future, that remains to be seen. I wait with baited breath, for time will tell!

Before I come to an end with this chapter, I would like to narrate some other Theta happenings.

I was up in Fonthill, in Canada, at one time last year. I was once again staying with my sister and brother-in-law, Marie and Pat, when my nephew David brought over Julie, his sweet young fiancée, to the house. All of the family had wanted to see what peculiarities lay about their own heads and shoulders, so I acknowledged all, to varying degrees of success.

David's girlfriend, Julie, was of French-Canadian extract and she had asked me also to take a look at her "paranormal peculiarities."

What I could see was a large flower, a tulip in the background just behind her head. There were a number of monks shown in the left segment that would indicate spirituality and a great white windmill in the right one. That intrigued me considerably, for there were now two symbols indicating a Dutch connection. I asked Julie straight out about what this Dutch connection to her was and she replied, quite surprised no less than I, that she was Dutch! Her father was Dutch, and that it was her mother who was the parent with the French-Canadian descent!

I should mention also that I have had experiences that one might consider to be past life regressions under Alice's tutelage, and they were, I have to say, of a most interesting character. On one occasion, Alice had me regress to a time to what I could only call the Celtic period, probably prior to the time any degree of Roman influence existed. I am inclined to believe that the area in question was Gaul, nowadays known as the Republic of France.

In my mind's eye, I saw myself clearly as some kind of physically disabled person with a type of impediment in my ability to converse correctly with other members of the tribe. I also was graced with a limp. I do not think that I was treated very well, and I would often retreat up onto a small hill to view a large dark green grove in the distance. The oaks that were growing close to the center of this grove stood out and towered well above all of the surrounding trees. It was by far my most favored place, and I probably spent much of my time there. On rare occasions I would return to the tribe's habitation close by in a small dell. The building itself proved to be very interesting and quite massive. It was circular, and made of wood, and had a very large conical roof, shaped like a cymbal, all made of straw.

When I entered the building I was totally ignored by all as the tribe went about their daily chores. Food was being prepared almost always as usual, while some loud discussion would continue unabated through the cries and boisterous hoopla of the young children, of which there were quite a few. The Righ, or the Rix in Gaulish, was the local king who presided over the opposite end of the building that was partly partitioned off to deal with those matters of "state," or whatever necessities it took to run a Celtic tribe.

I could see myself approaching the Righ at one time, only to be quickly and unceremoniously thrown out of the tribal building for my efforts. Obviously, I did not carry a whole lot of respect with my peers.

My final days came into my vision, and I was not at all very old when I passed away. I am standing alone on the hillock, the same hillock overlooking the large local grove. A tribal member is approaching in a threatening manner. I do not know him but he has his large sword drawn and he is waving it aloft and is exceedingly angry. All I can remember is seeing, in shock, my right arm on the ground, before another powerful strike takes me out of the picture for good.

It was the best of times and it was the worst of times; not on your life was it!

Using Theta, I will have to quickly admit, has been very enlightening and really, a lot of fun. It is a tool that can be used constructively and for the benefit of us all, and I am sure it is based on some old abilities that we have had in the past. Nevertheless, to consider Theta as some kind of holy gift given to us would have to be an incorrect assumption. It is a worldly tool and it is readily available to those who wish to learn to acknowledge its idiosyncrasies.

I have also found that it is up to about 90% effective in its abilities and capacity for 'healing' at its very best, which is about the result one should hope to achieve when working on this level of form. There is always that 10% that ego will insist on having control of, for magic is of its realm. By accepting this as 'healing', then, we are only unwittingly accepting ego as our overlord. Ego will emphasize and underline for us that we are not in any way in charge of any relevant problem, and that our efforts have not completely solved it. This cold insinuation suggests that the very same problem or affliction might return to flare up again. Therefore this is a farce, for magic can only be a temporary truce and as such, a brief hiatus. It is not in itself the full healing. We have to remember that ego does not care for us in any way at all; it hates us every way possible and pretends to be our friend. But with a friend like this, who would need such a dangerous and persistent enemy?

The Holy Spirit, on the other hand, creates His Own Miracles, where the whole perceived problem will simply disappear altogether by not accepting that there was a problem in the first place. This is a very important factor in realizing this condition, for all of the need for healing and release comes from the attributes of a very sick and unhealthy mind. A mind apart, alone, and not in unison with one's Guide, is one where the ego's mind-set will always hold sway.

Miracles are of the Realms of Holiness and are not indigenous to this, our level of form. So if a Miracle has been seen to have been accomplished on this level, it is because it has recognized that the problem did not exist in the first place. It must have encountered, addressed, and completely excised the whole notion that was but a miscreative extension of the sick mind.

Our old Dear Friend we have at hand and 'Guiding' publication, *A Course in Miracles*, declares that there is no level of difficulty when it comes to the working of Miracles. Miracles then must be of the Higher Mind or the Holy Spirit, which always has been and will remain a constant for us. And so the fluctuations and variations of necessity, ability, and strength are unimportant and do not pertain.

Miracles are immutable!

My biggest and only problem with the Theta healing was its phrase usage and application, where one needs to call on the Holy Spirit to do one's bidding. This is not, I think, a very efficacious way to heal as it is asking Him to make something on this level, which does not exist, real. The problem has not been perceived correctly, and then asking Him to take it away is an exercise in futility. Why on earth would He want to do that? For that would entail making the whole perceived notion a real event. But the Holy Spirit will never try to intervene on this, our worldly level, where a mind sees itself as still guilty and fearful and that, unfortunately, my friends, is how we generally do perceive ourselves. It is like using Him as some local preventative rather than the Cure.

The Holy Spirit does not try, in any way, to change all minds. He only influences and corrects the forgiving, accepting, and healing minds, He is working backward toward the present from our "end of time" debacle and our forgiveness, then releases all of the past's future inflictions. So what is taken up and forgiven in the past releases future perceived scripted lives.

Magic, dear readers, as opposed to Miracles, is the incomplete result of a mind in captivity, and thus a mind subject to ego. Miracles, on the other hand, are of a Mind that has embraced and is in total unison with True Holiness, a Mind that does not recognize apartness and separation. Always remember this.

Raymond Pratt
Nollaig 2006

Chapter 7
Original Sin or Original Innocence?

A long time ago, when God decided to create this world, or so the story is told, as narrated in the Book of Genesis, He decided to create man also, and in His very Own Image. This was to be a simple and straightforward Bible story as one can imagine, and also one that would hold for us all but a tiny smidgen of truth. God saw that the man He "created," namely Adam, was a little lonely and needed a mate in order to keep him company on earth. That name Adam (Adohm) was also, incidentally, the old Hebrew word for the color red. It most probably pertained to the color of the earth or rocks that were most significant in availability to the locale of the first man's habitation. It may have also represented the very same red earth that God picked up in His Hand to create man and to breathe life into.

When God decided to create a woman for Adam, He did a most peculiar thing. He put Adam into a deep sleep and created a woman from one of his ribs.

In all of the Scriptures there always seems to exist a tiny kernel of truth that just keeps on recurring ad infinitum. Yes, it does say that God took Adam and put him into a deep sleep, but then there is absolutely no mention or any record of God waking Adam up again! This is a rather surprising and unexpected situation for us, as it has to raise a number of relevant questions that need to be answered.

The point I am trying to make clear is that if Adam did not wake up again, then we can only surmise that everything that happened from that moment on, was and continues to be part of a dream. And it all does seem to correspond very closely to this world of ego where there is nothing real anyway. This, you can understand, will be an important observation for all of us as this was to be the first disobedient act by man to God's commands. It was accomplished, it would seem to us, all in Adam's dream world, for was he not still asleep and for the most part probably dreaming? Was he not dreaming of exile like we ourselves continue to do so today?

I know that this is all an exercise in semantics, but if our antecedent, Adam, was then fast asleep, under what law could he be punished? To me, it just all seems a little incongruent and trivial.

It is because of this first perceived "sin," then, that man and woman saw themselves cast out of the Garden of Eden with the added injurious insult of guilt, strife, shame, loss, pain, and ultimately death. Can we not by now understand that there is something vaguely familiar with all of these supposed recommendations for Adam's and Eve's dismissal? Does this look like God, our Father in heaven, paying what is justly and fairly due? This, my friends, does not look like the God we know and love at all now, does it? It is from these very early but faulty beginnings that dogmatic Christian thought is brought to its sad fruition.

It is by the same fruit of this tree that something will be found to be sadly lacking in bringing any contentment or peace to our brothers in need. This is the place where those ugly, misinformed, and overused words, "Original Sin," hold redemption to us as a carrot on a stick where one may or may not be forgiven.

Readers, let me make it plain and simple to you, for there is NO original sin and even if there was, would the Father hold us strictly accountable for something that happened to our long-lost misguided relative? Original sin suggests that an original mistake was made in the beginning. If God created something faulty, then the fault exists and extends from within Him. Fortunately this cannot be the case, simply because God is perfect and so are all of His creations.

Much of our Christian belief is based on the idea of baptism. This immersion in the water, holy or otherwise, partially or fully, is supposed to cleanse away all of our "original sin" that tends to undermine our final return to the Father. This is a most unenlightened and distinctly peculiar form of thought; it is as if our Father in Heaven would honestly try to place restrictions on the return of His loved ones.

When John the Baptist was offering his baptizing in the River Jordan to all who wished it, he did not use the term original sin but rather he suggested our immediate need for repentance. Because to repent is to "change your mind" (the Greek word is "metanoeite") in a new and correct direction, and to sin then, is only to "miss the mark" or so as to speak. Yeshua's followers in the beginning did baptize as John did, but the Scriptures were fairly quick to point out that Yeshua Himself did not do so! Nor is there any specific mention in the Holy Scriptures of the notion of any kind of original sin as the Church would have us believe. The exception might then possibly concern the "Red Heifer" sacrifice which (of which we shall talk of later) was offered on one summit of the Mount of Olives, beside the city's Temple Mount (Har HaBayit) on Mount Moriah.

The idea also of an occasional "scapegoat" being released by the Temple's high priests into the Judean desert at certain times represented the cleansing of the Israelites' cumulative sin, not original sin. So, then, for the Jewish people, there was no perpetual stain that baptism needed to remove.

It would stand to reason that the notion of original sin, in its present form, then must be a creation of the early Christian Church. Yeshua does not mention it anywhere I know of, for this may be more like unto the later Pauline doctrine and dogma than what the original Teacher taught. A most unfortunate time began where the original teachings of Yeshua began to lose all of their flexibility and inclusiveness, only to shapelessly crystallize beyond our immediate recognition.

In all probability, the peculiar notion of original sin started with St. Augustine of Hippo's doctrine. In his book, The Gifts of the Jews, Thomas Cahill mentions that one of Augustine's sources was from King David's remarks, after he was rebuked by the prophet Nathan. This happened after David had sent the general of his household guard, Uriah the Hittite, to a certain death after coveting his wife, Bathsheba. Bathsheba would be, eventually, the mother of Solomon and the builder of the first Temple.

David, now distraught because of his sin, prayed to God for

forgiveness and in his touching prayer included these lines:

"Behold, I was shapen in iniquity; and in sin did my mother conceive me."

This is one of Augustine's sources, but David's own words would probably stem from the common ancient assumption that human beings are evil.

Thomas Cahill also mentions that there was a famous proverb of the Sumerians and this is where Abraham's clan originated. The Sumerians existed in the year 3200 B.C.E. and their proverb states:

"Never has a sinless child been born."

So the question that we have to ask ourselves now is, was it original sin or was it original innocence that we were born with?

Yeshua tries to teach us to see only the present in our brother, for it invokes a holy exercise in perceiving the guiltlessness and innocence in him. The sad thought that our brother is, or could be, held hostage to the past of any kind by original sin is not seeing him as he really is. And if we cannot then see our brother as he really is, we have again blinded ourselves, for we cannot see what we ourselves truly are.

Our origins do not begin, nor have ever begun, in sin, for we existed long before the thought of sin could arise. Our initial creation by the Perfect One in heaven, who originally created our soul in the spirit world, is and remains the complete Extension of Perfection. So can Perfection be sinful? Can Perfection be seen to "miss the mark"?

All souls are innocent and their joyful innocence is a shameless reflection of their own particular Originality in the Godhead.

Belief in original sin is man trying again fruitlessly to find the original cause of his "guilt," and one has to agree that this would be a most convenient way to do so. The only problem is that this is what ego wants from us, for it will never let us be guilt-free, well, not for very long. Ego continually tries to keep us in its close charge this way, if it can, and because of this it feeds a special need for us to suffer, ergo original sin.

Original sin, in any form of reproach, is simply not a sustain-able notion for it is our original innocence that the Father sees, and innocent is what we are.

Raymond Pratt
Nollaig 2006

Chapter 8
The Godhead, A Trinity of One

*T*oday I am going to discuss, in some detail, how the nature of the Holy Trinity is perceived. Generally, in Christian traditions, the Holy Trinity is seen as three divine persons in the one God, each being equal in all ways and having existed from the beginning of creation. Other notions perceive this Trinity as three distinct entities, separate but with various interactive ties, as for instance in the LDS idea of the Godhead. Then there is the tradition of Judaism, which has many aspects and names for the Godhead, seventy-two that I know of, some of which we will attend to shortly.

As you can imagine, Judeo-Christian beliefs in God explore a certain commonality that can be expected as all monotheistic middle-eastern belief systems are firmly rooted in Mosaic Law. This being so, Christianity, Islam, and Judaism are all irrevocably entwined in the belief of the One Creator. This novel idea of there existing only one Creator was a great advance in ancient thinking processes and a correction of age-old customs. Take a look at the ancient but fairly common custom of keeping a plethora of generally benign gods in the household, cluttering up the family abode. There was prevalence for such idols in which the learned Greeks and Romans harbored no small esteem.

Judaism, probably the oldest form of monotheism, although based on the belief of the one God, had many names for the Creator, which were considered aspects and succinct facets of the Divine: El, Eloah, Elohim, Shekinah, El Shaddai, Ha Shem, Ruach Ha Kodesh, and YHVH to mention a few, and more recently, Adonai and Elohenu, which have been used together. We will now try to comprehend the nature of these names a little.

EL: This is the name for the one God, which comes from the Hebrew letters aleph and lamed that make up the two symbols of the ox and staff. The letters together symbolize the staff being used as a yoke for the ox. The ox and the staff when working on their own get nothing accomplished, but together, the power of the ox is harnessed and stepped down to work for mankind.

When Moses left the children of Israel to their own devices, as he climbed Mount Sinai, a golden calf (ox?) was created in his absence. Was it not the priestly Aaron who allowed this seemingly idolatrous situation to arise, as Moses had been on the mountain for quite some time at this stage? However, it does show that now Yahweh wanted to be seen in a different light and to break away understandably from the aleph/ox mindset that had been prevalent in His people's thinking. For this reason alone it would not be quite correct to say that the Israelites were practicing any idolatry because of their previous aleph/ox connections. Remember the Israelite nation had been, by this time, denizens in the land of Egypt for at least three hundred years or more. They probably had incorporated some of the Egyptian deities in their belief system, of which the bull played a prominent part. It then stands to reason, too, that to be a Hebrew slave would suggest that God had at one time or another abandoned them and could even now do so.

ELOAH: The word intimates the idea of one but not more than two presences. It was common practice to harness another younger ox to the yoke so that more experience could be gained for it, if you wish, a kind of god in training. Another notion was of ELOAH being YHVH and the Shekinah, or the Divine Presence where the Shekinah also had female connotations and the connotation of fire. It was used much more so in the Old Testament. One derivative of the Presence can be seen in Catholic churches, when the holy Host is kept in a repository known as the tabernacle; a red votive lamp burns close by to symbolize this Holy Presence. In all synagogues, a similar light, known as the Nehr Tameed, burns in close proximity to the repository of the sacred scrolls, which symbolizes the eternity of God.

ELOHIM: The plural of EL, the accompanying verb is always written in the singular tense, but meaning greater than one and not more than three. This is commonly used in the Old Testament and is where the idea of the Divine Trinity is finally incorporated into Christianity e.g. the Father, Son, and Holy Spirit.

EL SHADDAI: The Almighty or All Sufficient.

HA SHEM: The There or the Existence.

RUACH HA KODESH: The Holy or Sanctified Spirit or, more literally, the Holy Breath or the Divine Wind. Incidentally, the word "Divine Wind" crops up also in Japanese. It was the powerful and destructive wind that blew certain potential invaders off course, hundreds of years ago, from the coasts of Japan and to their doom. You will recognize the word for its recent usage as KAMIKAZE.

YHVH: The unspoken or unpronounced name of the Most High.

ADONAI: The plural of Adon, which means Master or Lord. It has the same connotation as the Greek word KYRIOS.

ELOHENU: Common nowadays and used with the word Adonai in most Jewish prayers and blessings. It means Our God. An example of such a blessing would be the following: "Baruch Atah, Adonai Elohenu, Melech Ha'Olam vuh Hatov Vihamayteev." The translation being "Blessed are You, Lord our God, Ruler of the universe and the Source of All Good." This completes some standard explanations of the many different faces of God in the Holy Trinity, and there are, of course, many others. There is also the notion that the Holy Spirit comes to us bearing some nine gifts that are conducive to finding our way home. But the Catholic Church insists on only seven gifts in total. These fruits of the Holy Spirit can be found quite easily in any of the New Testaments, Galatians 5:22-23 and are in English and Hebrew shown here:

Self-control	Shlitah
Meekness	Emunah
Faith	Atzmeet
Grace (as in goodness)	Anavah
Peace	Shalom
Generosity	Chesed
Long-suffering	Nedivoot
Joy	Orech
and	
Love	Ahavah

The book, *A Course in Miracles* brings us a step closer to the real meaning of what the Trinity stands for. How we, ourselves, are included as a distinct part of it is of supreme importance; however, it is not necessarily comprehendible to all on this level of perception but on the level of corrected thinking. This level of which I am speaking about is the one true nature of our being; it brings us back to the Sonship, the Second Person of the Trinity. This means we are an integral part of the Trinity, and Yeshua, our Brother, was, is, and will remain our path. Yeshua is the Way while the Holy Spirit initiates the journey. He is our Pillar of Fire.

So there it is, the Creator at Home waiting for us, eternally patient, and in case we forget the way, Yeshua, our brother, reminds us and shows it. Finally the Holy Spirit corrects all our base perceptions with Truth and Reality, and away we go home!

The idea that we are part of the Holy Trinity is quite a distinct and novel one and can, as such, make people a little perturbed. We are not comfortable in ourselves with the eternal aspect. We are constantly trying to find ways to prove our unworthiness of God's gift, and this plays straight into the hands of our old friend, ego. Our "friend" ego is in no way a respecter of our soon to be corrected belief system and has a million and one ways to "prove" a point, if ever a point has to be proven its way. However, if we are going to consider the following aspiration as true,

"There is only God
And God is,
I am made in His Image,
I am simply Love"

then whatever ego has to offer is proportionately false. Ego is no fool, however. Although it cannot understand the higher thinking of the Holy Spirit, it most certainly will be aware that something is amiss, which could very well be an insurmountable threat to its own existence in the end.

Yeshua and ourselves alone make up the Sonship or the Second Person of the Holy Trinity. We all have incarnated here on Earth, probably more than once. The only difference between Yeshua, our brother, and us is that He incarnated to demonstrate the all-pervading, reciprocal, and eternal Love of Our Father. It is through the Indomitable Compassion of Yeshua that the Way Home is found. We, on the other hand, incarnate out of fear and the misconception that we are guilty and most unworthy of forgiveness. Forgiveness for what and from who has never been the point, however, for the idea of guilt creates fear, which ego uses as ammunition to halt our advance. Ego does not want us to go Home and will prove in no "uncertain" way that our Home is here, a fallacy from beginning to end. The Sonship and the Holy Spirit are the only practical Way Home. Everything else is meaningless!

The Third Person of the Trinity is the Holy Spirit, who was created well before we left our Home through some misguided idea that we could exist outside God's Love. He is the life raft given to us by the Creator, the First person of the Holy Trinity, and available well before the very microsecond that we thought we could have been lost. This is His true Gift of Love. God knew we could never be lost because He only creates eternal Love, and we, no matter what, are His eternal creations.

It should be understood that we can always find our way Home through the Second and Third Persons in the Holy Trinity, using the right intention and frame of mind. So what about the Creator, Who happens to be the First Person of the Holy Trinity?

Another thing that we must not ever forget is that this whole nonsensical charade is not really happening. They are only but a motley collection of idle dreams in a sleeping mind. The truth of the matter is that, to God, we are fast asleep and dreaming of exile.

But let us explore a little further the workings of revelation.

A Course in Miracles does mention that a direct connection with the Creator is not readily available to us. But it is relayed via the Sonship or through the Holy Spirit, which are, for all practicable purposes for us, extensions of God, with all His capabilities. These extensions exist and were indeed created to be used by God's misguided creations, namely us! And if these extensions were created for us, then it would stand to reason that intercession is a necessary part of the connection to the Father. That of course, is not to say that intercession is always needed. Let's take, for instance, the famous New Testament parable of the prodigal son. Now this is where God's Revelation does take a hand. As the wayward and forlorn son begins to approach his father's abode, the father sees him in the distance. Overcome now with emotion, he rushes out to meet him.

Likewise when we deem to approach our Reality, the Creator encounters us for the last portion of the long and arduous journey. A truly awesome prospect awaits us where AWE could only be the one acceptable word to be used singularly for such a mind-opening experience of coming close to the "EHYAH ASHER EHYAH." These were the Hebrew words for that famous sentence that was spoken to us long ago on Mount Sinai:

"I AM THAT I AM."

Raymond Pratt
Aibrean 2006

Chapter 9
Lifetimes Interconnected

It was a cold, wintry, overcast day for the ninth of February 1986 in the US military hospital located in the small hillside town of Landstuhl, Germany. My wife at the time and soul mate of sorts was pregnant with our second son, Brendan.

Ciaran and Cristin, our first son and only daughter respectively, had also been born a few years earlier in Germany.

Brendan's birth was different in many respects. For the prospective astrologer, he was a noon child with the sun shining down from the mid-heaven position on the top of his birth chart; I knew that his sense of presence, as he got older, would be formidable to all in his vicinity. Added factors like the major conjunctions to the other planets at the mid-heaven, with the sun, would make for a most complicated personality. However, it is true that the "stars do not compel but only incline" so what's there to worry about?

The one little thing that I have left out here is that Brendan was born during the exact perihelion (nearest point to the Sun) of Halley's Comet. This comet graces our part of the solar system once every seventy-six years, and the last spectacular pass had been made in the year of 1910, when my maternal grandfather, Edward O'Kane, was all of thirteen years old. Perihelion is the term that puts the comet exactly behind the sun, sharing the same conjunction aspects with the other planets also. A rare and impressive sight!

Do these aspects make for originality, eccentricity, impetuousness, or contrariness? Not necessarily, but more than likely the person will display some of these tendencies. People born with comets in their birth chart in this position do need observation, for there is another old adage that says "when comets are seen in the sky, kingdoms fall." This generally refers to the kings of old that ruled. However, an Aquarian Sun placed high in a birth chart like this can show extreme eccentricities and very anti-establishment tendencies in the "stellium" of planets shown. (A stellium is a grouping of astrological bodies as can be seen on the birth chart.)

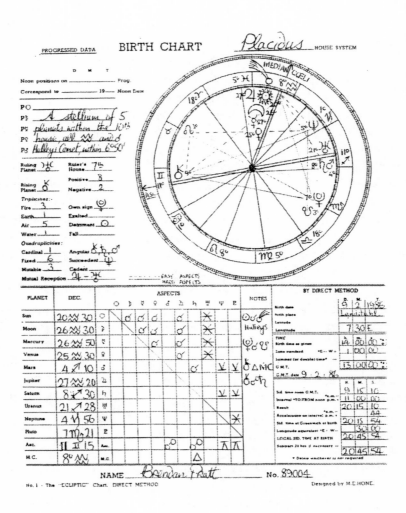

Brendan is an "old" soul; well, at least old for me because I seem to know him from someplace long ago. I have always believed that when my children were born, I would have to be there with my life's partner for some loving encouragement and to show a little sympathy by sharing the trauma. I have always warmed to the idea of assisting at births and had done so previously; for the whole not knowing is debilitating, and you know how the devil makes work for idle hands.

It was during Brendan's arrival, and I was holding the baby as they were cutting the umbilical cord. I felt a sudden jolt of recognizance slam through my head.

"My God, I know this little guy from somewhere!"

This would be the one and only time that it would happen to me with all the children. I remember Brendan, as a baby, loved to be carried on my back in Argentina, lording it over all, in his blue carry sack, his blond shock of hair standing up defiant and punk-like. He would grow up fast through his Utah adolescence, always being close to me, even during the very, very acrimonious divorce from his mom, a divorce devoid of any repair or reconciliation. Then a few short months after his nineteenth birthday, he would take the very same path of his older brother, Ciaran, and cease to have any contact with me at all. A sad state of affairs and indeed one that still needs to be ameliorated!

It was just around the same time in April 2005 when I was delving into the intricacies of Theta Healing that I had a most unusual encounter. Using my Theta teacher, Alice, we decided to experiment with the possibility of a past life regression. This is an area in New Age interests that I found fascinating and worthy of more study. I now had a chance to experiment and become the ready and willing accomplice of Alice's unscheduled regression of yours truly.

It is considered that all perceived "truth" pertaining to previous historical happenings in our history and our various existences are stored in the Akashic Record. The record can also be considered a reasonably private affair, for there is certain information that is not supposed to be available to just anyone, or so it is said. However, I had very little difficulty in obtaining what I wanted. I imagine the record is available for perceived closely tied networks of souls, but in actual fact, souls are all of one creation. Being so close to Brendan, I decided to try and find out if both of us shared existences in earlier lives, and if so, where and when. Nevertheless, the results of my peculiar search would shock me more than just a little!

Alice asks me to lie comfortably on the floor and to meditate for a little. She then asks me to imagine myself in a field following a pathway. As I walk down this path, I notice a gazebo slightly to my left in the distance and I can see some kind of entity within, illuminated slightly.

As I approach, the entity looks more like how I would perceive an angel. The only problem is that he (for I did assume he was a he) says nothing and although he looks like he should be endowed with wings, he has no such appendages visible. I feel like he is some kind of guardian, and he begins to accompany me a little off to my left side, toward a large set of polished wooden gates. He bids me to enter mentally; I do so only to find him standing to the left of a plain stone altar bathed in a soft pink light; in fact the whole room is bathed in this light. Alice then asks me to reach under the frontispiece of the heavy capstone protruding from the altar. I do so and quickly find a small, bright, silver key and bring it over to another recessed and smaller, heavy wooden door adorned with slightly open drapes, to the back and right of the altar. I enter and continue down a slight decline, proceeding through low arches, each lit up with one of the rainbow colors, all shining with a relatively subdued light.

And lo and behold! I find myself standing on top of a partially elevated stone wall that reminds me of low battlements; I feel the warm, bright sunlight of an early summer's day warming my back while I face northward, looking at the emerging scene.

I am overlooking a very green pastoral landscape sparsely dotted with what I think are compact villas and tall, gracefully narrow trees. I see great swathes of open meadowland, and I have the distinct certainty that I am in northern Italy. Glancing down at my feet, I can see that I am wearing sandals and my legs are bare. I notice also that I am wearing some kind of common white tunic that comes down to my knees. I am a Roman or possibly an Italian of some description, and I do feel that I am in my younger teenage years.

Alice asks me quietly to turn to my left.

I do so quickly, only to see a younger male child with black hair, about eight years old. He is dressed exactly like myself and he has this peculiar and quizzical smile on his face as though I should recognize him. I know instinctively somehow that this is my brother!

"Catullus!" I shout out to him in my mind's eye.

However, all this was a little too much for me! So I mentally retreated back up the same way I came, up the rainbow arches, replacing the key hurriedly underneath the capstone, and then I made a hurried exit. It simply was too much information!

It was only later that this same novel information I was allowed to glean would seem to pay off in a large dividend. It would emerge for me in the form of known Roman historical documentation and my ability to find and access it.

Previously, Brendan, Brian, Cristin, and I had gone to see Pamela Roberts, an acquaintance of mine and a talented psychic who was demonstrating her abilities to a class of about twenty. During her demonstration she tried to focus on specific questions asked to the Other Side. Pamela had given some thought to Brendan's presence, and he may have had a question to ask also. She saw that he was extremely well-endowed with the gift of writing, music, and poetry, something I wasn't aware of. I, naturally thinking that she was off-track, thought she was picking up on my abilities. But no! So much for my ego! She was very adamant, and I filed this incident in the back of my mind. I never thought that I would be able to use this information she had at a later date.

I decided to find some more information on the name Catullus. The first entry that came up for me was of Gaius Valerius Catullus, a poet of great renown in ancient Rome at the time of the consul, Julius Caesar, and the rapidly expanding Roman Republic.

Julius Caesar was to be the victor and scourge of the Gauls, and was the one who captured their king, Vercingetorix.

Catullus was born around 84 B.C., the younger son of a wealthy citizen of Verona. They did own a country villa at Sirmio on Lake Garda. Naturally you might think that these places are located in northern Italy, and yes, they most certainly are. Catullus knew Cicero and they were known to be friends. It is also well documented that his older brother traveled through Asia Minor and Bithynia, areas that had recently come under the control of the Roman Republic. These areas are now located in modern day Turkey.

Catullus's poetry was of the popular Alexandria school, which was inherently Greek and proved to be quite appealing for its content and vigor. It was joyful, earthy, and sensual, and it could be very sincere and touching. Nevertheless, Catullus did not live very long and by the age of thirty-one or thirty-two, he was dead.

Catullus's life, although short and meteoric, was in some ways a dissipated and trying existence. He was always in and out of love affairs and secret trysts, but he had an older brother whom he loved very dearly. This brother, probably no more than seven or eight years older than Catullus, even loaned out his house to him on many occasions during his amorous shenanigans, and his name was Allius Manius.

Allius Manius would be the older loving brother of Catullus that I would eventually have to associate my previous existence with. Allius would also have to play an important supporting role in the life of Catullus, and we only know this from the famous poem Catullus wrote for his departed brother. This was written on Allius's untimely death, probably around the year 62 B.C. when he was about thirty years old.

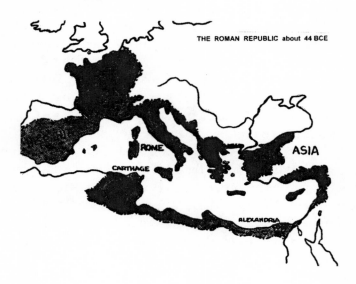

THE ROMAN REPUBLIC about 44 BCE

Allius was on a trip to the old city of Troy, in Asia Minor, when he fell into water and was drowned. This would have a devastating effect on Catullus, but it would empower him to write his most momentous eulogy to his dead brother. After completing the long journey to the scene of his desolation, this eulogy, as one that could only be written from the heart, would be the masterpiece that he would be forever remembered by. The poem is called "At the Tomb of his Brother" and here are some excerpts:

> I cannot, O ye goddesses, refrain from
> Telling what the matter was in which
> Allius helped me and how greatly he
> Helped me by his services, lest time
> Flying with forgetful ages hide,
> In blind night, this kindly zeal of his...
> And let him be famous more and more
> In death; Let not the spider who weaves
> Her thin web aloft, spread her work
> Over the neglected name of Allius...

> Atque in perpetuum, frater, ave atque vale!
> And forever, brother, hail and farewell!

I have forgotten to mention that I do have a fourth son, who back in 1989 was my only son to be born in the city of Limerick, in Ireland and we named him Cathal. Its meaning pertains to "battle worthiness" or "mighty in battle." It comes from the word "Cath," which means "war" or "battle" in the old Gaelic or Erse language. This name Cathal, does sound fairly close to the Latin name of "Catullus," but it may also show my preference for a name or names that may go back many, many lifetimes.

I, dear reader, have up to now failed to inform you convincingly or even adequately of why I may think that I might be the future incarnation of the older brother of Catullus, Allius Manius.

In my own mind I was able to identify the general northern Italian location and possibly, the topography of the family home. I did indeed see myself as the older brother and by that relevant age gap.

I have also, I will have to admit, greatly suffered from a severe case of wanderlust. This is a trait readily seen in the far travels of Allius to Asia Minor, then a relatively new province. This area now covers a substantial part of modern day western Turkey that during this time, had been recently incorporated in the Roman Republic. I have also failed to mention to you, honest reader, that I loathe the thought of, and am absolutely terrified of being under water. This is the only unreasonable fear that I can safely say I have, and to this day, I have never learned to swim!

Raymond Pratt
Meitheamh 2006

Chapter 10
And What About Judas Iscariot?

*H*aving a sympathetic understanding of the nature of Judas Iscariot, the so-called betrayer of Yeshua in the garden of Gethsemane, needs a little additional thought and consideration by us. Perhaps we should remember that Judas Iscariot was an Apostle and one of the twelve original Apostles to be chosen by Yeshua. These twelve would happen to be the nucleus and harbingers needed to bring Yeshua's message to the local populace. This being so, then each and every one of the Apostles would have to have a particularly significant part to consider in promoting the Rabbi's plan. It is very obvious that we cannot really be quite sure what His plan was for all of the Apostles. But it would be inconceivable to honestly think that Yeshua could use one of His chosen twelve to be His "hated" betrayer without He, Himself being totally aware of it. Aware of this He most certainly was, and if that was the case, the consequences then had to be part of His original scheme.

Judas's second name, Iscariot, may have come from two different sources, which we will try to explore. The word "Iscariot" could simply be the corruption of the word "Kerioth," as in "Ish Kerioth," which could pertain to a small hamlet in Judea, not too far from Jerusalem. The "ish" word pertains to a man in Hebrew and probably in the old Aramaic, which was a language akin to Hebrew. So the name "Judas Ish Kerioth" would mean "Judas, man of Kerioth."

The name could be also a corruption of the Roman word "Sicarii," and that is the name given to the Jewish zealots who were an incessant thorn in the side of the Roman occupying forces. The name stems from the fact that these zealots would carry daggers concealed by the voluminous cloaks that they wore. It was not an unusual case to see these zealots endeavoring to foment various incidents of a vicious and bloody nature that would then aggravate the Romans. This was their resultant plan, for they in turn wanted the populace to stage an uprising. They would create a distraction in the crowded streets to cover the planned murder of one or two of the Roman soldiers in the process of carrying out crowd control. The narrow side streets that were available for pursuit by the Romans were traps that could then swallow them up. Here, any effort by anyone to follow the Sicarii would be very dangerous and probably deadly. In effect, the Sicarii assassins were a kind of terror weapon of their day, as they struck when least expected.

Judas also may have been the quartermaster or paymaster for this little group, as it seems that he was the only Judean among all the other Galilean Apostles. He may have been more street smart and savvy to the ways and wiles of life lived in the largest city, Jerusalem. The city was an infrequent stop-over point for Yeshua and His little group, for He generally retired to Bethany, on the other side of the Mount of Olives at the end of the day. Judas was also quite vocal and highly critical of the use of expensive and exotic balms that were being used on Yeshua's feet prior to His Crucifixion. He commanded a very intimate knowledge of how much these valuable balms would cost if resold.

Judas was very wise in the ways of the world, but he probably was and had to be the necessary grounding pole for this little esoteric group. This little group, we have to remember, were distinctly and understandably simple people and looked upon by Judeans as country bumpkins. They were unaccustomed to the city's ways and new lifestyle that their loving Master was initiating them into.

Could Judas be ever forgiven the deed that he was associated with, which brought about the demise of His Teacher?

First, to accomplish such a task would make him one of the most hated beings that ever lived, for it begs for a few other questions to be asked also. Did Judas do this willingly? Did he want to bring an end to Yeshua's role, for such an attitude would bring a sudden end to his assumed and "privileged" position? Or did he do it unwillingly; in other words, did Yeshua request this as a favor of him? If this favor was asked of him, it would be a disheartening self-sacrificial exercise for His Teacher on his behalf. It would also bring a tremendous burden to carry in the form of guilt. However, we must remember that Yeshua's plain and simple teachings did not invoke or ever imply guilt, so this scenario is highly suspect.

It is unfortunate that we are always inclined to see first the more sinister side of people's ulterior motives. Whatever agenda Judas had, I am quite positive it did not include the gruesome sight of his teacher, Yeshua, hanging on the cross, lifeless. And who knows what excruciating mental agony and suffering that this poor misguided man had to live through in his final hours before his suicide. What catastrophic thoughts and guilt did Judas contemplate on, where in his ultimate dismay, the final horrifying results of his misdirected intentions began to play out?

If he did it willingly, was he in his right mind, or was he simply inebriated? After all, it was the holiday season and at the end of that day's particular accomplishments. Who wouldn't care to sit down for a little supper and a few rounds of wine with a number of one's well-chosen friends? It would seem, too, that thirty pieces of silver will not buy you a whole lot more than maybe a small derelict field to hang yourself in. Anyway it is assumed that he did return all the money to its original owners, whether it be the Romans or the Sanhedrin. All this, and still to be completely torn apart with regret and remorse would be too much for any man.

Judas Iscariot has been, and will remain for now, a scapegoat, a reason to blame a brother lost in some obscure maze. A reason to project hatred and perceive guilt on an errant creation of our Father in Heaven, all for the satisfaction we think it will bring us. Are we not also "guilty" by dissociation of similar and likeminded thoughtlessness?

Even the word "scapegoat" is in itself a peculiarity, both unique and well documented in Judaism, which pertains to the absolving of sin. Every so often it was known that the Jewish priests would initiate a ceremony and take a goat, purportedly carrying and retaining the sins of all the Israelites, and release it with their sins into the Judean desert. This, in effect, would temporarily cleanse the whole Jewish nation of its own notion of sin and guilty conscience until it had to be repeated again at a later date.

Yeshua had proven to all at this point how He could forgive anything and anybody. His forgiveness was all-encompassing and non-exclusive. But if there had been any final and culminating lesson at all to be learned by Him, what would it be? Could it, or would it not have been the total forgiveness needed for that unloved and lonely, unfortunate miscreant, that universally hated and perdition-bound "traitor" in His camp? The burial place of Judas is supposedly (H)Akeldama in the Hinnom Valley.

Raymond Pratt
Mean Fomhair 2006

Chapter 11
The Unreality of Time

*E*very day that we spend here within this very trying existence is calculated and measured. It is fruitlessly spent urging ourselves readily forward to catch up with our perceived wants and needs. The Lord knows we are, indeed, truly needy creatures with such impaired tunnel vision. We are so particularly endowed and cursed with such insatiable appetites that they have no recognizable end in view. We are, in a sense, like those old Buddhist "hungry ghosts" that you will read about in the book, Bardo Thodol (The Tibetan Book of Living and Dying). The wraiths pertain to those who, in the ancient Tibetan lore, prowl the earth and lower astral planes, never being able to be satisfied.

We wake up fresh in the morning and from there plan our wayward and oftentimes misdirected lives with absolutely no compunction to ask why. This we do as though we own this passion-locked piece of not-so-real estate that we deem to call Earth.

Everything we try to accomplish here with our lives kowtows to the rule of time, and this lordship is, and can only be, one of the domains of our old shipmate, ego. That perhaps, you think, may be all very well. But if we really were aware of what ego's hidden agenda was, and how it planned to use it, we would then well understand our particular cause for concern.

We do seem to have a limited existence that insists on being filled with a plethora of various unnecessary schedules, and of a seemingly important nature. Those insane schedules vie for our immediate attention and beg to be completed, no matter what. As such then, the demands called for on our time evidently play out to be an endless, petty game of charades.

But wait just one second, who is it that is deciding on what needs to be accomplished in the first place? Is it that little nagging doubt in our head that keeps all of us running around in circles? Or is it our monkey mind syndrome? Or is it part of our own pride and self-esteem that seems to be cajoled, needled, or fawned upon by the maudlin attempts of the illusory ego? Could it possibly be that we are being led astray?

Let's be straight and honest about all this! This is solely the work of that old sycophant ego again. It wants us to believe that there are endless arrays of things we need to worry about, for the time that we seem to have available to us. But, unfortunately for us, that will always be the case. It is purely a trick, with the sole intention of keeping our minds off what our real quest should be. And it is done with the strict intention of trying to dissuade us from the Pure Truth of our Real Teacher, the Holy Spirit.

Yes, time and space also were created by our very own cooperation with ego. But we were not ever meant to be made privy to our partner's artful shenanigans. We were not meant to be consulted in any way, nor were we to be considered in any matters, for any reason at all. Therefore, this unholy union bears all the symptoms and thought processes of a demagogue in charge, and thus should not be heeded.

Nevertheless, the Holy Spirit, in His own quiet way, uses all of these miscreations that we have absolutely no earthly need of. He is infinitely resourceful, and like some divine Gardener weeding, takes what I call the compost in our lives and uses it in a constructive and instructive manner. This He can do to great effect, while at the very same time, undoing and undermining effectively the ultimate plan of attack that ego surely has hidden for us.

Ego's secret plan involves how we perceive our past and future. We don't always see the future with our rose-tinted glasses, regardless of whether its results are beneficial or detrimental. That, in essence, should not bother us in the slightest, for all it is, is ego's duality in action, and we must beware the machinations of the split mind. And generally speaking, whatever result ego has managed to obtain, it probably had a plan, or some other kind of built-in countermeasure for an opposite result anyway. Otherwise it would not be living up to its well-earned title, the Lord of Duality.

Have you ever noted the anomaly in how we tend to divide actual time? This is something that is constantly being overlooked by us. We tend to divide all perceived time into past, present, and future, but have we noted that the segments are very unevenly divided?

And guess who the ruler of division is?

The most glaring anomaly that lies before us is the fact that the present has no measurable timeline at all. In actuality, it would seem that it does not even exist. And if it does exist at all, to any small degree, it must exist as a small sliver, a tiny wafer-thin border between the past and the future. This, for us, happens to be a very, very important observation and I will tell you why.

The past holds for us all of the "good" and all of the "bad" situations that have arisen in this life and previous lives. It is only perception, though, and ego wants us to retain all of those bad experiences. For it is through our retaining these experiences that ego manipulates the submission necessary to enhance our guilt through the element of fear. If the guilt and fear happen to be carried over through this life from the past into a perceived future, it will have a detrimental effect. It will surface as self-loathing or possibly project hatred onto an innocent brother, for both past and future are the different sides of the same coin. Duality in motion, and this is a result that ego will find all too satisfactory!

Remember, we scripted this "movie" with ego a long time ago, and so the past remains one of the most potent weapons in ego's vast armory. An arsenal fully stocked with various disinformation and misinformation bombs. The script agreed upon can be reworked and edited by using the present as a focal point. But for now, past and future will continue to remain as the paltry, desiccated, and embattled wastelands of the lord of time, provided we want it to remain that way.

Now let's talk about the present!

The present is about where we are at any given spot in time. It is hardly measurable and that is because it exists only as a tar strip connecting the Past to Future highway. It was indeed created to be so small as to be almost immeasurable for a very particular reason. But within this little crack that is tarred over and hidden is a secret that will promote our last and most important journey home to the Father. This little secret will freeze over the past/future timeline and set the clock back to zero and permanently in the present. By setting the clock's hand back at zero to the "Holy Instant" moment;

"The past then ceases to inflict a future on us that is wholly unnecessary, and thus it fails to materialize."

It just does not exist. All that is left for us is the ever present, the now, the always, and that, my brothers and sisters, is the portal of the "Holy Instant." When we stop perceiving time simply as some function of our lower mind, The Holy Instant occurs and we see our brother in his true light, timeless and innocent. He is without a past or a need for a future incarnate, for his salvation is our salvation and this Holy Instant portrays what he is.

Our function in this life on earth is to heal through the power of the Holy Spirit, or Yeshua if you wish. The only real option we have is to heal, nothing else! Healing with pure love for our brothers and sisters ultimately endorses healing in ourselves. But all this is done from the "present" or "now" standpoint without any regard for a past. So we need to see our brother guilt-free and with no association to any kind of past.

What I need to stress from the last paragraphs is that the past MUST be forgotten. In honesty, the past simply does not exist and an emphasis on someone's past record will not bode well for our own speedy return to our Parent. So all healing must be completed with absolutely no regard to any previous detrimental history perceived in any of God's creations.

It is only the past that insists on us with a future ruled by Fate, and what is fate but ego in another one of his disguises? To be ruled by fate is to accept our "guilt" and live an existence where the gods (ego again) are the rulers and deciders of our "fate." And this is simply incorrect thinking, for every one of God's creations is guiltless, holy and innocent. We have to believe that they are inviolate and holy. For what the Lord God, our Father, creates from His Holy Perfection has to be holy and guilt-free. This is regardless of whether we or they are aware of it or not.

The present is where God and His holy creations coalesce. It is the "treffpunkt" or meeting point for pure spirit conjoined. It is that place where we all finally go home together.

What we must continue to do is to prize apart the past and the future. This is where we take the off ramp on the Past Future highway marked NOW. We have no need of the past or a future that does not include all of us on the return journey home to our Parent.

"And the more that we are aware of the present, the more of 'The Presence' (HaShem) will be made aware to us." (As a "Holy Instant.")

Time does not really exist, and so for this reason neither do the past and future exist. That leaves only the present, which exists as a kind of launch pad for our salvation. For is not our brother our own salvation and are we not here to forgive and heal him, and by doing this, heal ourselves also?

When God spoke to Moses on the mountain, He was speaking from the eternal realms where the past and the future would hold no meaning to Him. A mind preoccupied with the past, breeds fearfulness and cannot exude holiness. And as for a mind focused on the future, this is a mind dreaming dreams within a dream. The heavenly realms only exist in the now, and in a sense that would make the "present" or the "now" especially holy in its own way! So the mind fixed in the present has all the potential for holiness, for it is a mind gazing into eternity.

What was it that God said to Moses when asked His Name? He did not give a history of Himself and say,

"I was what I was."

Nor did He suggest any self-improvement, or a need for it by saying,

"I will be what I will be."

God used the present tense to underline a simple tenet to emphasize the now and the always, He said:

"EHYAH ASHER EHYAH" or "I AM WHAT I AM."

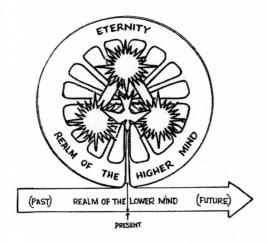

On the illustration shown here, we now can easily see the God-head of the Trinity. Superimposed upon the Trinity is an aspect of God that is always available and can be called into action anytime. That is, of course, the Holy Spirit, Who on many occasions is symbolized as a dove. Encircling the Godhead is man's higher aspiration and eternal mind, where within the constant emanations of the Great Rays (from *A Course in Miracles*) of the Godhead are interacting. This higher mind incorporates that which God had always planned for us. Below this circle shown is the timeline that extends from the past into the future by the arrow moving from the left toward the right. This is the region of the lower mind where we perceive only the past, present, and future. There is a point where the higher mind and the lower mind touch at a tangential point, which emphasizes that man's plans are not God's plan. This point is the present or the "NOW" where the Holy Spirit can be accessed. As can be seen plainly here, very little of those divine rays penetrate across to the lower mind, but enough do so to initiate our journey home through the Holy Spirit.

Raymond Pratt
Deireadh Fomhair 2006

Chapter 12
The Jerusalem Journal + February 2006

*O*ne of the most convenient things about working for an airline is the availability of cheap travel. Even with the high government and security taxes that need to be paid, it tends to be a fairly decent bonus. The only real downside to this is, of course, the fact that you only travel if there is an available spare seat onboard, a rare enough commodity these days!

It was in February 2006 that I decided I would take a trip to Israel/Palestine/Holy Land; this was something I had always wanted to do. Family opinion, being what it was and still is, considered me to be absolutely nuts. What with the suicide bombings and the whole general security situation in Israel, how was I ever going to find the ability to see anything? Naturally, being the wayward and fearless wayfarer that I am, I was very determined to stick to my guns and prove to the family that all was safe there. That is, of course, provided one is to follow some very simple, basic precautions. I also managed to discreetly elicit a tacit promise from my mother back in Ireland, for she had always wanted to visit Israel, that she would accompany me there on a later trip. That was, of course, based on the fact that I, naturally, returned safely home without anything of a prominent nature missing.

So that fateful February Saturday morning, I started my trip to Tel Aviv (English for Spring Hill). I was to route from my home here now in Salt Lake City, Utah through Delta's Atlanta hub and then on to Frankfurt. The flight to Atlanta was uneventful, and after a short delay, and being comfortably ensconced on Delta's 777 in business class, we took off on the transatlantic trip.

Just a little while later, over the Raleigh/Durham area we had a little problem where all the cockpit lights started blinking, so back to Atlanta we went.

Shortly after, we would use another Boeing 777, but the delay meant that I was now definitely going to miss my Lufthansa flight in Frankfurt. And as such, I would not be landing in Tel Aviv that following afternoon.

Arriving at the Frankfurt airport about ten minutes after my prospective flight had departed; I was left with the rather unsavory idea of spending a whole twelve hours here on a winter Sunday. Twelve hours in this German airport on any God-given winter Sunday is not fun. It is about just as interesting as being trapped on Shabbat in the ultra-orthodox Mea Shearim (Hebrew for 100 Gates) district of west Jerusalem. A whole lot of nothing to do (at least you better not be doing anything!) and nowhere to go, if you happen to be an uninformed gentile. So I resigned myself to being bored out of "mein kopf."

Tempus fugit, but not in this case!

After that mighty ordeal, I truly welcomed the idea of some rigorous security checks to break the grinding monotony. I found that the Lufthansa agent, impeccably groomed and friendly, had given me all of three seats to the back in the central aisle of the new Airbus A-330. Whether this was done because she knew I would be drinking some very palatable German Warsteiner beer along with a tasty lamb curry, I don't know. But I'm sure she herself was probably not well acquainted with the profound effects of the mixture of what I was going to be eating and drinking. Still, the gesture was very nice and it was considerate of her to offer those seats, and the food was very tasty, all the same.

Four hours and a time zone later, I see the orange lights of Tel Aviv off to my left as I prepare to make my very first landing in Asia. It is about 3 a.m. in the morning, and everything goes as well as can be expected through customs and immigration. As I enter the very new and cavernous arrivals hall, a plain-clothed and relatively friendly securocrat pulls me aside to ask why I am in Israel. Do you have friends in Israel, have you any family here, are you Jewish? The questions went on and on. I reminded him, jokingly of course, that I had a Christian Hajj to accomplish and surprised him in our dialogue when I told him that one of his own previous presidents, namely Chaim Herzog, was born in Ireland. So with a few choice remarks about Ireland's historical contribution to world-wide presidents, and a friendly nod and wave from him, I took my leave. Now, I had entered the ancient and fascinating land of Eretz Yisrael, or, if you wish, simply Ha'aretz (Hebrew for "The Land") to your everyday folk here.

I was totally gaspers for a café-au-lait, so I jauntily sauntered (or is it sauntily jauntered?) over to the local coffee shop, and in the best Irish-American Hebrew that would ever assault the locals' ears, I asked confidently for the local holy nectar. I asked:

"Ana rotzseh café nes eem khalav kham! Bevakasha!"

As you can imagine, this perfect rendition had them hopping all over the place. Believe it? Not on your life! Perfecting the way to ask for a Nescafe made with hot milk could seriously hinder the amount of time left for my vacation. All in all, though, I found that they were a sporting bunch and were quick to smile at my bungled attempts at Eevreet (Hebrew for Hebrew).

Israel is blessed with many innovations, but the one that rises to the occasion is the sheroot. The sheroot is a cross between a taxi and a hotel shuttle for roughly the same price as the set fare on a bus. They do make many stops but are relatively cheap, so I had planned to go straight to Jerusalem on one. However, as for buses at this time of the early morning, there aren't any. Trying to find a spare sheroot at 3.30 in the morning was just another unneeded obstacle that was proving to be just as insurmountable!

It must be pointed out here also that the potential for one's first major blunder can rear its all too frequent and embarrassing head. The plural word for sheroot is sherootim, but this word sherootim ALSO means toilets or washrooms. This is the case because the word does actually translate into "services."

So continuing on my futile quest for transportation of the cheaper variety, I was befriended by a lonely taxi driver in need of a last fare for the night. We both settled on a price that we thought, or should I say he thought, was pretty reasonable and we then headed for the Judean hill country where Israel's capital, Jerusalem is magnificently located. The air temperature down in the Sharon plain for February, where the main airport is located, was very pleasant. One could hardly think of the weather here as winter.

I will be honest with you, though; my driver did intrigue me as I thought that he was a bit of an odd fish and he looked like he was going to fall asleep at any time. At one of the stoplights, he failed to drive off as the lights turned to green, and I had to offer to drive the rest of the way for him. He countered that I didn't know the way. Hah! That was laughable as there is really only one highway into Jerusalem and it alone serves as the only highway there from anywhere to the west of the city. Later my driver did stop on the side of the main highway only when he saw a Hasidim man's car broken down. After finishing his Good Samaritan work (I don't know if he would appreciate the metaphor) we slowly continued through the night to the ancient city. I found that Israelis are quite helpful with each other but in a nice offhand way so as not to suggest a favor having been done. The element of spontaneity to help was refreshing and, I think, based on their strong socialist leanings that were inherent and necessary in the founding of their state in 1947.

About 4:30 we did arrive ay the outskirts of what seemed to be a rather newish but very hilly city with absolutely no movement of any type going on. This was the new Jewish capital, the city of West Jerusalem. This is where the Knesset, the Israeli parliament, meets, and a short drive on further east found us approaching the famous Jaffa Gate (Hebrew is Sha'ar Yafo) of the old city. We continued around by the city's northern wall to where the Palestinian Arab areas began in earnest, and I took my leave of my driver.

My driver had some grave misgivings, well, maybe not quite so grave, about leaving me off and alone at the Damascus Gate (Hebrew is Sha'ar Shechem). It was still very dark and this was a heavily populated Arab area. But this was the nearest city gate to my very reasonably priced Arab-owned hostel, the awesome "Al Hashimi," which was located in the heart of the Muslim quarter. I headed off down the steps and through the arch of the Damascus Gate. Down I went, meandering through the narrow, twisting, and cobblestoned streets with just a vague hint of the smell of refuse and a slight twinge of apprehension in the air. I hoped that both would not prove to be too overpowering! Anyone I did see in the streets, I offered a "Sabah a'Noor," and in general, it elicited a positive response from them on more than one occasion. For it was then that I found that the more the local inhabitants answered me, the more I felt at ease. Mind you, I was probably still murdering their poor Arabic language like I did with the Hebrew spoken back at Ben Gurion airport!

A few short minutes of rapid walking in unison to the thump-thumping leitmotif of my Samsonite suitcase on the damp cobble-stones, and then I was there. I found myself outside the door of the Al Hashimi hostel on the exceedingly narrow Suq Khan ez-Zeit street. I started pounding on the hostel's door all to no avail, but the sky was getting a little lighter now. I turned round and sat down resignedly on the stoop to watch the build-up of early morning passersby. After a little while, perhaps fifteen minutes at best, a backpacking Australian early riser making a hasty exit offered the open door to me and in I went.

I climbed up what looked like some wide marble stairs and took over a hard wooden and very ornate seat in the small high foyer, which looked vaguely like an interior courtyard. Later I was to find that the building was about 500 years old and built in the time of Turkish Sultan Suleiman the Magnificent, the same Suleiman who rebuilt the city walls in the fifteenth century. After about a half an hour the hostel began reluctantly to come alive, and I was then introduced to Saim and his extended family, and they all proved to be very friendly and helpful. I indulged myself in a much-needed hot shower (and surprisingly, it was hot!) and went back upstairs for a superb breakfast that included a tasty mushroom omelet and the best black plum jam I had ever tasted on toast. The breakfast room with the not too talkative Dutch chef overlooked the Dome of the Rock, this being the same place where the Jewish Temple of 70 A.D was destroyed. That, of course, had been foretold to all by our Lord Yeshua about forty years earlier, during His Ministry.

But who could believe that I could find a room with this mind-numbing view on hand, and all this to be had, with breakfast included as well, for $25? And that's not including the rich and engaging experiences I would have forever. Just absolutely marvelous!

The very first thing I had promised to do for myself on arrival here was to take the Via Dolorosa (Latin for the Sorrowful Way) to the Church of the Holy Sepulcher. It lay roughly about a five-minute walk through a 2,000-year-old labyrinth of narrow lanes and was located in the Christian Quarter. A little later that morning I headed up toward the Holy Sepulcher church, but it proved to be such a daunting ordeal. The street sellers' very loud and strident invocations for one to sample their wares were overpowering. The calls were friendly and alluring but quite often demanding. Quite often I felt like I had to navigate my path like some old tramp steamship, unable to stop even if the urge was there, and to a rising and insistent cacophony of calls in my wake.

In the end the Holy Sepulcher would remain an anomaly, for I could not find even the faintest whiff of holiness or sanctity about this place. It remained for me only as a dark, confusing labyrinth of dark, medieval rooms and passages that reminded me of the dark Machiavellian minds that created it in the first place. There were some peculiar stories about Adam's skull having been found when excavating underneath the presumed Crucifixion place here. That, for me, was the final straw and from there on I took a wide berth of the Holy Sepulcher. The stories about Constantine's mother, Helena, and what she found in the fourth century on her pilgrimage here are both quite bizarre in nature and understandably Byzantine.

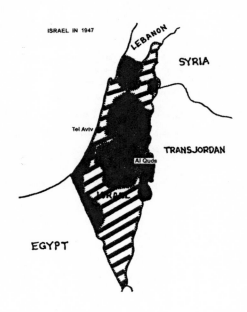

Jerusalem was not as warm as the coastal plain, for it is in the hills, so I quickly decided to visit the Dead Sea area (Hebrew is Yam Hamulkh, the Sea of Salt). This region lies up to 1,500 feet below sea level, has ten percent more oxygen in the air, and is decidedly warmer. It takes only a half an hour to drive down to that level where, through irrigation, bananas and dates grow profligately in large plantations. After I had asked a fellow passenger at the bus stop discreetly for directions to the bus station, I waved down a No. 6 bus, and I said to the bus driver,

"Ha'im yesh ha'autobus shesh b'takhanah merkaveet, adonee?"

He was having none of that. The poor man must have thought I was an alien from the deepest regions of Upper Slobdonia from the directions I was now almost shouting at him in his native language. But all things come to an end and, thank God, I did locate a bus for Masada Rock on the second or third floor of the main bus station! Please don't get me wrong, for the people in general were particularly friendly and quite helpful, but it was the odd occasional character that I would meet that added spice to my experiences.

I was one of the last to board the green Egged bus for Masada, beside the Dead Sea, and found my seat half occupied by my neighbor. He was absolutely massive but I did manage to squeeze into my seat. After a solemn descent down to the sea with my neighbor snoring like a saw, we passed the stop for Qumran. Qumran is where the Dead Sea Scrolls were found during the last century and was an Essene stronghold. The next stop was at the oasis En Gedi, a beautiful watering hole where King Saul stopped to take a pee while trying to chase down and kill his successor, David, of Goliath fame. David had been hiding there and could have killed the king if he had wanted to, but obviously, he refrained from doing so.

Finally I got talking to my neighbor. He was an ex-Australian sheepherder of the Jewish faith who wanted to settle down here. When Jewish people feel a need to resettle in Israel, the government will always help them out considerably, and this program is called "aliyah," a kind of returning home. This means that if a Jew from abroad at any time feels he is being persecuted or in any way treated differently, he has the convenient option of another home.

By the time I had reached my stop at Masada Rock, my new acquaintance had offered to put me up at his seaport home and vacation spot in Elat on the Red Sea. That was about 150 miles further on, unfortunately, to the south and it would just have to wait for another expedition.

Masada was superb! What with all that extra oxygen in the air I decided to ascend the mountain by the Snake Path, and in fifty short minutes I had reached the very top. I had also walked in on the swearing-in ceremony that the Israeli Defense Forces held here for all of their new recruits. The white and blue striped Star of David flag was fluttering in the breeze like a prayer shawl, and this is where the army swears its special oath of allegiance that Masada will never fall again. We must remember that Masada held out for two years against the Romans during the insurrection that would include the complete destruction of Jerusalem, both city and Temple. After it looked like the Roman army would finally succeed with their two-year assault on the mountaintop fortress, the whole group of 1,000 people, men, women, and children all committed mass suicide save for the six who had hidden away. The earthen ramp that the Romans built in 72 A.D. specifically to subdue Masada can still be seen rising up on the west side of the mountain.

The views here were wondrous, across the salt sea to where the mountains of Moab darkly rose up into the Jordanian sky.

My trip back to Jerusalem later was uneventful so I decided to avail of a cheap Armenian restaurant where the food was hot and plentiful and the beer, cold. So after a fulfilling day in all respects, I started my traipse home through the dark laneways to the yowl of the fairly substantial cat population. I saw five filthy-looking cats in the alley; I swear they looked like they were honestly having a feline conversation. Two of them were engaged in intimate nuzzling. The other looked like it was ready to stop traffic with one hind leg high in the air while, with diligent use of its pink tongue, it blatantly continued to nurse its prominently displayed unmentionables. While all this was going on, two more cats came up with their own obscenely funny version of social pleasantries; it was like some kind of perverse Rotary Club meeting. The whole charade could only have me in tears laughing all my way home.

Hey! And no, I only had two bottles of beer!

The next day was damp and proved to be quite cold with the very rare promise, would you believe, of snow. The locals insisted on telling me that they had plenty of snowplows in any event. Yes, they had! I hoped all four snowplows would be in first-class working order as Jerusalem, with 650,000 souls, is the largest city in Israel! Anyway I was spared this would-be remarkable sight for the weather then turned mild overnight.

Walking the city walls proved to be interesting, too, as I got to meet children, Christian, Jewish, and Moslem all playing happily in their schools and backyards. They were all asking my name and where was I from.

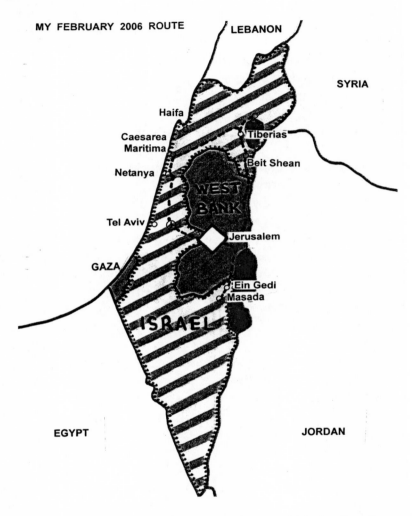

Jerusalem is a city of "katzen, kirchen und kinder," a city most definitely of hilarious cats, odd churches, and feisty children. However, as I approached the compound of the Dome of the Rock past St. Stephens Gate, some Moslem children started to throw some pebbles at me. A shout from a guard on the compound wall of the Dome reminded me that I was getting way too close to their holy place. I then turned round and retraced my steps without much further ado.

Shopping in the new city of West Jerusalem, which is mainly Jewish, was a pleasant experience compared to shopping in the alleyways of the old city. Prices tended to be very reasonable, especially in those little huckster shops, and I got some really good bargains. It is a real shame that we don't have these kinds of old stores in the USA anymore. I suppose profit margins demanded nowadays are not large enough to be of interest for the stockbrokers.

On my second to last day in Jerusalem, I decided to take a leisurely walk around to the east side of old city. I was now staying at the Terra Sancta, an incredibly clean Christian hostel run by the Franciscans. However, the Palestinian hostel staff, although friendly enough, endorsed favoritism and on occasions acted like little Hitlers, especially at mealtimes.

I ambled slowly down the hill toward the Garden of Gethsemane (Gan HaShemanim, meaning the Garden of the Olive Presses). It is overlooked by the Golden or Mercy Gate that leads straight into the Dome of the Rock compound. This gate was sealed up by the Muslims a long time ago, as it was considered the gate through which Yeshua entered the city for His last Passover. The Muslims then interred bodies in graves there for a very special reason. They wanted to forestall any Second Coming and triumphal entrance by Yeshua and what better way? They also saw Yeshua as a rabbi, and it is known that religious Jews do not cross over graves!

Take a look at an illustration of the Kidron Valley; if you can draw a line from the sacrificial site of the Red Heifer on top of the Mount of Olives all the way through to the Mercy or Beautiful Gate, it most probably lined up with the main entry steps of the original Jewish Temple (Hebrew is Har HaBayit for The Temple Mount) of the first century. But Jerusalem is a city of speculation and as so, so are my deductions.

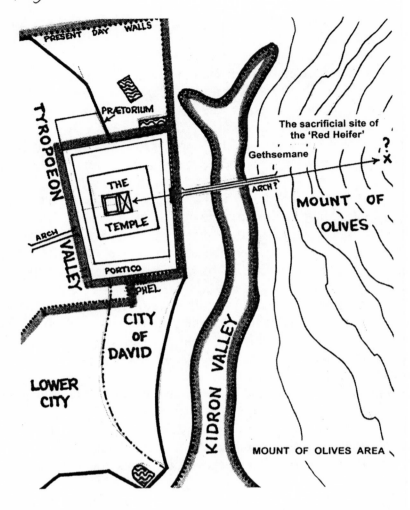

Another day passes quickly and it is now time to take my leave, so about midday I try again to catch that familiar No. 6 bus to the main bus station, and succeed. My green Egged bus will now whiz me off down onto the plain where my ELAL plane is waiting to whisk me off to New York. At a secondary stop en route, a young chap boards the bus; I guess he must have been about the Bar Mitzvah age, roughly twelve. There are only six people on the bus and he decides to sit by me, and he is going to the city of Pet-wah Tikvah, near the Ben Gurion airport where his grandparents live. It's scary enough to think about suicide bombers on civilian buses, but he must have been told by his parents to sit beside an adult. Fortunately, he being Canadian, we had a good deal to talk about.

Night is approaching and I get to board the third Boeing 747 heading for the New York area. The agents were very sweet and totally accommodating, and again I managed to get three seats to myself, one being a window seat.

We begin our take-off roll and I am thinking of the other two 747s that have taken off before. It reminds me of the story of the three soldiers on the front line who wanted to take a smoke. The first soldier lights up and is seen by the enemy. The second soldier also lights up and the enemy takes a bead on him. The third soldier lights up, BANG! And you're dead.

As we take off I am straining my neck to see out on any launch of missiles against us from the West Bank a few miles away. And that's a sad ending to my trip, the fact that it would have to end by making fear real. But not one that would stop my mom or me from returning to this wonderful place and friendly, intriguing people, all of three months later.

Raymond Pratt
Deireadh Fomhair 2006

Chapter 13
The Holy Trinity and the Jewish Qabbalah

An interesting example in trying to find another way to understand the Holy Godhead can be found by the use of the Jewish Qabbalah based on the "Tree of Life" method. This is a unique type of esoteric discernment that was, for quite some time and still is, used by successive mystics. Many of these mystics of mainly Jewish extraction found it to be exceedingly worthwhile to study, especially in looking a little deeper and further into the workings of the Heavenly Realms and man's purpose thereof.

The Tree of Life diagram of the Qabbalah shows ten spheres called sefirah (sefirot is the plural, in Hebrew, for spheres). They all have very different names that envision different qualities, worldly and otherwise. There is also a secret sefirah situated over the Abyss, which sits slightly below the three upper sefirot. This sphere is known as the "Da'ath."

The Abyss divides the Heavens above (En Sof) from the mundane of the earth below. This then represents the gap between the limitless and eternal, and the lower realm that remains subject to the limiting time-space continuum. The top three spheres are representations of the Godhead or the Holy Trinity while all of man's far-off worldly dreams, temporary creations and manifestations are represented by the lower spheres.

Our central sphere placed right in the middle of the illustration provided, "Tiferet," symbolizes abstract beauty, and is located on the lower middle path of the Tree of Life. It tries to represent what a higher-minded man can ascend to, unwittingly without the quiet help from his Divine Mentor, and this is about as far as man can proceed in this world of duality. Any concept of further advancement up the Tree of Life from Tiferet necessitates a Divine Intervention from Yeshua, our Brother situated at the Binah sefirah or by our Guide, the Holy Spirit at the Chokhmah sefirah, or indeed by a Direct Revelation.

The Direct Revelation method could only come and then very rarely from the Father's sefirah at Khether. Note that all the worldly pathways that emanate from the sefirah at Tiferet correspond solely to those special innate abilities of God's Creation, namely ourselves, trapped in exile and perceived apart! In other words, they do not really contribute to our important decision to return Home to the Father but may prolong our perceived separation.

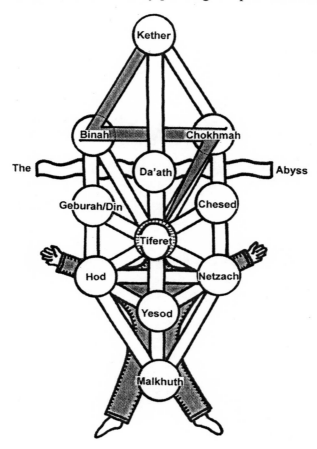

REVELATION & DIVINE INSPIRATION

As we have mentioned, Tiferet stands for beauty in its most abstract but worldly form. From this point, all of the paths are open to man with the exception of just one. The only path that leads directly to "Kheter," the Crown, crosses directly over the Abyss to the Father, but it is, for all practicable purposes, restricted solely to the actions of the Father upon His Creation. Here is a list of some of the qualities inherent in all ten sefirot:

KHETHER	Crown/Love	The Father
CHOKHMAH	Wisdom	The Holy Spirit
BINAH	Compassion	The Son
CHESED	Mercy	ditto
GEVURAH	Power	ditto
TIFERET	Beauty	Higher Self
NETZACH	Victory	ditto
HOD	Glory	ditto
YESOD	Dreams/Foundation	Man's desires
MALKHUTH	Kingdom/Roots	Tenacity

We must also consider that secret sefirah lying over the Abyss high in the Tree of Life illustration, for it does play a particularly important role between the Creator and man. To define this role, we use one word, Revelation:

DA'ATH	Abyss bridge	Revelation

The three upper sefirot are "Khether," the Creator and "Chokhmah" and "Binah," representing the different aspects of God if such differences could ever exist. I am inclined to believe that all of the various aspects associated with God are equal and interchangeable. They altogether symbolize the Trinity of One in the Holy Godhead of love, wisdom, and compassion respectively. These representations do come exceedingly close in our perception to those three distinct and interacting natures that we generally are aware of in the Holy Trinity.

Khether symbolizes the Creator above.

Chokhmah is the Knowing and the Certainty of the Holy Spirit. It is Wisdom, Reality, and, yes, the Paraclete bestowing the

Fire of Pure Truth.

Binah is the Messiah, the next step extended by the Creator to bring Home His creations. This would then be completed through the incarnation of Pure Compassion, Yeshua, our Brother.

When we draw a line between Khether, Chokhmah, Binah, and Tiferet, it suggests lightning or a thunderbolt, for it is Divine Inspiration grounding in the higher mind of man. The lightning bolt then must travel through Binah or Chokhmah first, for it does not really matter as both are interchangeable and the results will remain the same. It is interesting to note also that in *A Course in Miracles*, just in the beginning it mentions that we can use Yeshua OR the Holy Spirit to promote our spiritual journey Home, for both have connections to this level of existence. The other paths that emanate from Tiferet aim at man's more banal and peripheral "needs" with the exception of the path leading from Khether to Tiferet.

This path itself is unique, in so far that it leads across the Abyss to man, and this is where God the Father speaks through the unique and holy element of REVELATION. For most cases and in probably all, the path is one way and is, primarily, the Presence of the Creator reaching out to the soul that is particularly close to its Reality.

The position of the secret sefirah or sphere, "Da'ath," is situated on the central axis of the Tree of Life and below Binah and Chokhmah. I believe that the Da'ath position is a bridgehead between the Father and His creation, lying partly within the Kingdom and partly within our own dream of exile. It is a kind of temporal cum spiritual black hole or the Alpha/Omega point that I talk about in Time Correction. It is a bridge between time and eternity, if ever such a bridge could exist. As we approach it, for we all must eventually, our lives begin to change and take on a different focus.

It is only then that reality becomes Reality, the Omnipotent begins to fill and expand our ever widening horizon as all mundane notions of the ego are carried swiftly away on a whirlwind of revelation. This is, for all purposes, what we only need and nothing else. The Supreme Compassion of Yeshua allies with the Holy Spirit's Burning Fire of Truth to immolate us completely in the eternal Love of the Father. This, my friends, is our Reality!

Without Binah and Chokhmah, namely the Son and the Spirit, we could never have found our way Home. For both have done, do, and will always intercede to the Father for us at the Khether sefirah. If we had to wait for Divine Revelation itself, instead of the Divine Inspiration offered to us, it would take such a very long time to return Home. Intercession would be generally out of the question and Revelation, being of the Father, would be that much so rarer. However, this would never be the case, for the Father loves all of His Creations and He is aware, unlike us, that we never left His Presence in the first place!

Da'ath plays an important part here as all temporal manifestations become what they really should be; a brace of dreams, smoke, and mirrors. Here man, now endorsing the central path, gives up the fallacy of duality in any form. No male/female conundrum, no good/bad, no time/space, no positive/negative, nothing in flux or formation, nothing but Oneness and Love.

This is the point where the Father sees His son in the distance and rushes out to meet His prodigal and wayward progeny whom he could never, ever at any time condemn; He then stretches His Arms across the dividing Abyss and finally embraces His son, who has woken up finally to his Reality, forever. The lost sheep is found! But was he ever lost to start?

Man's blueprint has, on many occasions before, been wrongly perceived as tattered and torn, but it must have incorporated in it succinct vestiges of his Creator. When we become aware of what we really are, we have made the decision to start the return journey Home like the Prodigal Son. So the journey down the road to cross the Abyss is what we should all be working toward. But let there be no doubt in our minds at all, we ALL return Home in the end. It just could not be any other way, for with the Father what belongs to God ultimately and unquestionably returns to Him!

Raymond Pratt
Meitheamh 2006

Chapter 14
Remembering God

*Y*es, it is true that we do grow up being used to the idea of fulfilling our expected religious duties on Sundays, As Sabd (Islamic) or Shabbat. We learn all the necessities of our basic belief systems and genuinely anticipate and hope for any chance in promulgating worthwhile deeds. These will be attended to, and by us, much more willingly completed on those very special occasions. For is there not always this compulsion inherent in us to impart and underline our basic need to be seen as consistently good followers of the One Lord God?

However, let's be honest with ourselves for a change and try to comprehend what all this time with God should be about, as it is generally inclined to take a backseat in our everyday and busy lives. And that's all very well, just as long as we are comfortable and compliant with our very own "backseat driver," but who can in all honesty say that they are?

Why do we need to "remember" God?

Should we suppose that our religious obligations, which we endeavor to complete on a weekly basis, are to be of a sufficient nature and to everyone's satisfaction, no matter how, where, and why we pray? Surely God should find such ongoing duties that we perform to be adequate in His Holy Remembrance. Ego would have us see it, after taking everything into consideration, as a manifestation of the perpetual encumbrance it generally does feel to be to us.

But God is not about religion, and remembering God is most certainly not about our paying lip service to rote, form, or deed. It definitely is not about the need for our fellow brothers and sisters to be indoctrinated, nor is it meant to be about having to perform any kind of perennial religious obligations scrupulously nor sanctimoniously.

It is not about the type of scriptures or quasi-official "sacred" writings that we endeavor to study whether our tastes lean toward the words of the Bible, Torah, or for that matter, the Qu'ran. Nor is it about our need to practice asceticism or to emulate the lives of those past spiritual masters of humankind, although they may certainly help to put us on the right track.

Remembering God is about giving consideration to our very unique connection to our Parent in Heaven. He has been trying to catch our wandering attention ever since the day that we perceived our departure and exile from Him. Our remembrance of God should then be based on acknowledging Him and by accepting this we empower ourselves. We can arrange this successfully by removing the accumulated clutter of all the manipulations, all those blocks, veils, smoke and mirrors that we use to hide from Him. It is about finally recognizing within ourselves and especially in our fellow man that particularly unique and spiritual origin that we all intimately share. Perhaps within our brother's and sister's release will lie this key to our very own salvation?

We cannot leave our brother to the wiles of ego. How is it that we could have unwittingly misunderstood those persevering and unwavering efforts of our Loving Parent incorrectly, and still, does He not continue to indulge us? Are we not so much like some little children sometimes? When we do not want to be disturbed or distracted in any way, we put our fingers in our ears while at the very same time drowning out any effective dialogue with some loud clamors of disapproval.

Yeshua DID say to us that we must become like little children before we can enter the Kingdom of God. This is something we all must be willing to do, by submitting and releasing completely our daily cares and distractions. And who better to submit them to other than the Holy Spirit, or if you wish, to the compassion of Yeshua or to our Loving Father by intercession.

Let "Them" look after our everyday needs, like some young child who feels protected in the midst of its doting parents. A child does not have to worry about yesterday, nor tomorrow, but only about what is going on in the here and now. And heaven is not about what has gone before us, nor is it about the future to come; it is simply about the now, the present, and the Kingdom within all of us that is not so very far from our grasp.

Yeshua also suggests to us that we should not ever be considering what the future brings, for a future implies a guilty past. So we must be like children, for they have no need to worry so much about such tiresome and petty, mundane matters like mortgage payments, fellowship, and health. It is by these constant worries that we make our temporal world very real and thus a major stumbling block in our lifelong search for the Kingdom within. And ego has planned it this way, no doubt.

Children will always thrive on a life based where their day to day needs are met, which is something that we need to consider. A child's attention span can only be in the here and now, and that is exactly where all of our focused attention for our Father should lie. Why should we pay any particular attention to the shallow pretensions of those tiresome illusions of future dreams, past defeats, and everyday living? Duality offers the same continuous option repeatedly, disguised as something new. The slim pickings offered on any level of form are unfulfilling and prove to be and are at best, scant. Let the remaining world of form go its own peculiar way, for we have a journey that we need to accomplish.

And think, to dream of this world is nothing. To dream of a tomorrow for this world is to dream within a dream, all in all a totally insignificant labor and a complete waste of time and effort.

How long will it take for us to finally accept that the distance we keep from our God is most definitely NOT of His doing? Every day we make the thoughtless and time-consuming decision to be distinct and apart from the Holy Spirit and Yeshua and, by extension, the Sonship. In doing this, our ignorance is at play and we are prolonging our gradual return to the Father's abode and delaying our own ultimate fulfillment. We consistently do this each and every time we are inclined to ignore those incessant promptings from the Voice and Remembrance within. Or indeed is it right, when we fail to act correctly upon seeing the plight of all our brothers' or sisters' urgent, burgeoning, and plaintive call for help?

What has been frequently placed before us always is an opportunity for holiness either in loving our brother or in showing true forgiveness to our brother. And all calls for help can only be a call for love and it is your holy function to respond!

Remembering God is seeing there in our neighbor the all-forgiving Face of Yeshua, or maybe it just might be that bright burning pillar of light within? Or is it the kindly hand offered at that very exact moment when needed? Truly the soul remains to this day as that brilliant and intense spark, a memory of its own creation, in each and every single one of God's Creations that can never, ever be extinguished. No! Not even by the grim machinations of ego's ultimate test and macabre gift to all of us, death itself!

I have taken an excerpt from Martin Buber's book, *Tales of the Hasidim: The Early Masters*, written in 1947, of what Rabbi Shmelke said to one of his very own disciples, who, being intent on improving his own spiritual condition, had asked about what he should do about loving his neighbor:

"Love your neighbor like something which you yourself are. For all souls are one. Each is a spark from the original soul and this soul is wholly inherent in all souls, just as your soul is in all members of your body. It may happen that your hand makes a mistake and hits you. But would you then take a stick and punish your hand because it lacked understanding and so increase your pain? It is the same if your neighbor, who is of one soul with you, wrongs you because he does not understand. If you punish him, you only hurt yourself."

This well-learned and uniquely compassionate rabbi, a most noble soul, had also this to say of the notion of loving "wicked" men:

"Don't you know that the original soul came out of the essence of God and that every human soul is a part of God? And will you have no mercy on Him, when you see that one of His holy sparks has been lost in a maze, and is almost stifled?"

Remember Yeshua, a loving incarnation and filial extension of the Father, and our Brother, did not come to prepare the way for the righteous but for the "sinner" and the outcast. After all there is no gain in being especially kind to family members or close friends, for this is only the spontaneous result of fellowship, and Yeshua points this out to us quite effectively in the New Testament. Yeshua was specifically sent here among us to light the way for those intermittent "lost cause" souls whose own eternal, but weak and flickering sparks were in dire need of His attention. So it is the guilty ones, the ones who project fear and a need to attack, who suffer for they have a need of Him. As for the guiltless, *A Course in Miracles* states:

"A guiltless mind cannot suffer."

So it is only natural that we can then warrant some unexpected provocations from our errant neighbors. We should only see them simply as a lesson in the essential learning experiences on our own road to forgiveness. For without them there is no salvation!

Remembering God is about remembering our fellow man, who was created likewise at the very same time as ourselves and therefore can only be equal in every aspect. It is for that reason alone that every single soul must be its own mirror image of the unified and conjoined soul that we always originally were, are, and will be. The whole thought of fear, guilt, separation, difference, and division can only be our own faulty projections of incorrect perceptions that obscure the real picture of our true nature. So are there then some souls that are more enlightened and special to God than others?

There are no old souls and likewise there can be no young souls. How could there be, for is not the notion of being young and being old illusions of time and therefore a nonessential necessity to what's eternal? Hence souls must then have been created altogether and at the same instant. To even consider or to aspire for a moment to the erroneous idea of being an old and experienced soul, a veteran of many lives, is to serve ego in its hierarchical domain. It is then that a need for a "special relationship" is implied. God most certainly has no special favors for any of us, for can we honestly imagine or believe for a moment any type of favoritism or exclusiveness existing in the singularity of Oneness?

Imagine this picture, if you wish, where all humankind exists as a kind of hologram of the Sonship. Every single soul having to share the very same abilities and Reality, to which they all have to ultimately aspire and awaken. An idea where every individual action performed then has the ability to bring all closer to their common home. This has to bring the self-awareness we have needed and our final redemption. I have taken what I consider to be a pertinent excerpt from our *A Course in Miracles* book, from chapter ten, the "End of Sickness," page 189. It talks clearly about the Mind/Soul concept that I find illuminating:

"The power of one mind can shine into another, because all of the lamps of God were lit by the same spark. It is everywhere and it is eternal. In many only the spark remains, for the Great Rays are obscured."

"Yet God has kept the spark alive so that the rays can never be completely forgotten. If you but see the little spark you will learn of the greater light, for the Rays are there unseen. Perceiving the spark will heal but knowing the light will create."

"Yet in the returning, the little light must be acknowledged first, for the separation was a descent from magnitude to littleness, but the spark is still as pure as the Great Light, because it is the remaining call of creation. Put all your faith in it, and God himself will answer you."

And if God Himself wishes to extend His Holy Person to answer us, this portent will blossom as possibly Divine Intervention or, on the rare occasion, pure Revelation. And Revelation is the Prodigal Son's final arrival at the borderlands of his Homeland. Those are the same borderlands where the Prodigal Son makes his long-awaited entry to his Father's abode, with his Father close beside him. Emanu 'EL! God is then with us, forever!

Raymond Pratt
Lunasa 2006

Chapter 15

Time Correction & How It Works

"When you perform a miracle, I will arrange both time and space to adjust to it. The miracle shortens time by collapsing it. This eliminates certain intervals within it. It does this within the larger temporal sequence." (*A Course in Miracles*)

*W*hat does the Holy Spirit mean by this statement? Does He mean that the time and space continuum can be manipulated on a different level to our benefit? After all, does not the Holy Spirit operate in the eternal, in a similar manner like the Father, and why should He worry about things of such a transient nature?

The time and space that He is talking about only concerns our existence on this level, the level of form. We are souls in turmoil subjected to all these self-made parameters due to the imperfect nature of our lower minds. We create, but all our creations are faulty and become, ultimately, victims of time. Consequently, even our existence itself, even as a part of the mundane, has a finite period that needs to be renovated after each successive lifetime. How many lifetimes can be counted from the dawn of our first physical existence here on this excuse for a home to the present? And just how many of these fruitless lifetimes are repetitions because we simply failed to forgive? If we only had an inkling of how supremely powerful and necessary this forgiveness process is!

So even if we have lived generous and constructive lives and have done our duty, so to speak, while there is an element of guilt, fear, shame, or envy, this will show as a debilitating flaw in our nature. And that flaw needs our immediate attention and correction. It really is of the utmost importance to understand that we cannot return Home, carrying some incomplete aspect of our present existence, at loggerheads with our brothers and sisters. To simply try and go Home without our brother or sister is tantamount to rejection of whom we all really are and therefore is not possible. Heaven is not a Home for you, me, or any other living soul until the true nature of our own beings begins to flower within. But flower and bloom it most certainly will, for this is the Wish of God our Father. And when God's Wish and our wish share this common strand, absolutely nothing can stand in Our Way.

Fortunately, the Father had already created a path out of this peculiar conundrum by His Own extension of Himself through the creation of the Holy Spirit, and that is all we need to clear our perceived "guilt." This loving extension of the Father needs only the true forgiveness that every one of us should readily have available for one another. For it is then that we turn our wavering attention to the job at hand, the return journey Home. How is this to be accomplished and can it be completed post haste?

During our many existences here on earth we have built up an inordinate amount of negativity that we have not released. If this negativity is not cleared completely within a given lifetime, it will ultimately become stored in an area of the consciousness where the subconscious acts as a release mechanism, frozen on hold. Through successive perceived lifetimes, the negativity will in no way be mitigated or diminished until acted upon. The negativity projected will then accumulate through the ages until there is the action needed by the Holy Spirit, who lifts it when we forgive. This subconscious that we talk about is part and parcel of our consciousness, which exists between all these lives lived and is also, yes, you've guessed it, an aspect of ego!

Any single thing that keeps us from going directly Home is ego's realm. So with the untimely demise of one existence for another, the lessons so urgently needed to be acted upon are now not readily accessible nor are they available to be considered, addressed, and finally completed. The lessons end up in the dark part of our consciousness, a very unwholesome place that finally will need cleansing before we return Home.

Without the help of the Holy Spirit we would never, ever be free of this dark labyrinth. Even if we could free ourselves, we would still have to deal with the Minotaur in the guise of ego, not that you would probably ever recognize it as such.

As we endeavor to forgive correctly, a miracle is created. This miracle will involve the removal of some perceived, subconsciously operated, previous nastiness embedded within, from during some earlier existences. Indeed, there is absolutely no order of difficulty for any kind of miracle involvement and healing when it comes to Divine Providence removing obstacles to our Return. He asks only for some input on our behalf, which would be our agreement to acknowledge for ourselves the total acceptance of the Atonement, which really means "at-one-ment" with our fellow man, an honest and open commitment to forgiveness. When these commitments are accepted unconditionally and acted upon diligently, we have then accepted the Atonement and thus are prepared for the Call Home.

"Do the Holy Spirit's work for you share in His function. As your function in Heaven is creation, so your function on earth is healing. God shares His function with you in Heaven, and the Holy Spirit shares His with you on earth." (*A Course in Miracles*)

So, all in all, what we intend to forgive here in our present existence can be forgiven totally through His succinct system of surrender and release, and readily available to all studying the wonderful book *A Course in Miracles*. The Holy Spirit, to sum it up, is our clearing house Agent, which simply means that if we forgive our brothers and sisters, living and passed over from this life, He will then obliterate the darker and uncomfortable aspects of our subconscious bit by bit. And the healing does not only extend from forgiving people, living and dead. Everyday situations such as sickness, headaches, anger, road rage, depression, anxieties, insomnia, the next-door neighbor's dog barking nightly, in fact just about ANYTHING that deprives us of peace should be forgiven and in doing so, certain traits will begin to unfold for us. These traits are at least twofold and will entail radical but very positive changes, at least, to our perception of fear and peace of mind.

Fear begins to disappear out of our lives. If one can imagine for a moment what life can feel like without the element of fear in it.

For me, it is like I am covered with a Teflon coating and anything that accosts me tends to glance off with no apparent detrimental effect. Trust me on this, ego will most certainly do its damnedest to you in every way possible to confront you with a multitude of potential troubles and then probably all at the same time so as to knock you off-balance. The troubles I find can be likened to a flight of arrows aimed at us, but as the arrows travel and traverse the intervening distance, they begin to turn into what I imagine as raindrops. Our perception slowly begins to change, culminating with an intense feeling of peace, invincibility that is lasting, and a harmonious and joyful appreciation of this wonderful gift. Now we have a really good reason to smile and be happy again. We can now proceed again and advance, for are we not wearing our new spiritual "body" armor that needs no physical weapon? For our foe is now disarmed, and his sword is ineffective, it is neutralized, forever transformed by love and Knowledge, all with compliments of the Holy Spirit Himself.

It was also during this period that I completed two trips to Israel within the short space of three months. These trips would include driving my Israeli rental car well into the Palestinian West Bank areas on my own and also with my mother on the second trip. This would include a trip to Hebron, a flashpoint city for Jews and Muslims and sacred to both because of Abraham and Sarah being interred there. Some might consider this as being reckless and foolhardy and a lack of foresight on our part. But how could we see danger from a brother or sister whose pathetic actions and reactions are a call for Love constantly? Remember, anger is always a call for Love! We could not ever have felt any kind of mistrust, fear, or trepidation during this time, only sympathy and an honest and deep compassion for both sides. It was sad to see so many fearful Israeli and Palestinian souls lost for many generations in their present dark morass of vituperative tit-for-tat aggression.

The other gift of the Holy Spirit that I have noticed also was a genuine feeling of peace of mind extending noticeably into the repetitive and the more mundane aspects of everyday living. I felt so much less for the need to fill up my life with pointless tasks, distracting endeavors, and the constant urge to entertain myself. At times, I felt as though I was trying very hard to run away from myself. Such distractions should all be considered as ongoing covert actions of a vicious ego trying in vain but earnestly attempting to stem the Voice within, the Voice calling me Home.

We need to pray, but what is equally important, too, is that we need to stop praying awhile and to embrace some quietude so that we can listen to the Voice inside, very probably trying to answer our prayer.

Another gift that I have noticed recently, which was not so very obvious to me at first, is what I call vision, but vision with a small "v." I should state now that I do not have any control over it as it just happens. But on five occasions so far, when faced with an unanswered question, or possibly a remark made out of fear by a family member or friend, I was given the whole result instantaneously. It was as though the present and future coalesced into one overriding end result timeframe. I really cannot explain from what part of my brain that this stems, for the answer was so clear and certain that it became a fait accompli before it even started. This is a good example that underlines the possibility of lives being scripted at another level. But no matter what, I will accept this gladly, but humbly, as a bona fide gift from the Holy Spirit.

A wonderful peace of mind also extends past my dealings with my divorced and estranged ex-wife and six children. Of course it was necessary to forgive them as soon as I could, which I did manage to do eventually, but I find that I do need to repeat this new forgiveness process on an occasional basis. Nobody thought that it would be easy, but the ultimate benefits of this kind of constructive forgiveness do far outweigh the very little inconvenience for me. Some other members of my side of the family find this forgiving process rather peculiar, goody-two-shoeish, and out of context. But then again if there is anything that can help us to attain especially at this level a little peace, should we honestly care what people think? Our peace will finally extend out and bring them their peace also!

It is for this reason alone that I am convinced wholeheartedly that I am doing the only correct thing available to me! So now we know some of the results brought about by our forgiveness; let's talk about the mechanics of these miracles.

Probably the best way to understand and be aware of "time correction" is to have just a little knowledge of Yeshua's famous parable of the Prodigal Son. We take our leave of the Father on a very unnecessary journey albeit by our own choice. This decision to leave really is the Alpha point of Yeshua's saying,

"I am the Alpha and the Omega."

TIME CORRECTION

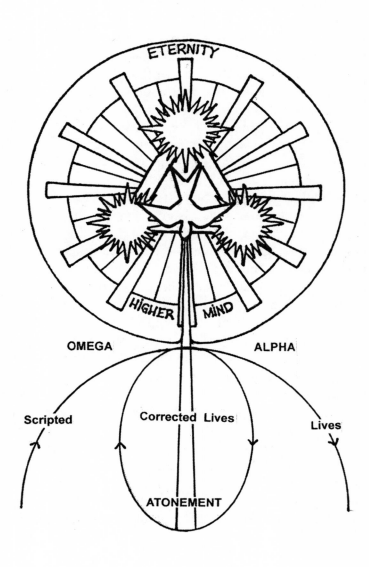

The Omega point is also in the same place as the Alpha point. Why? Because both points do represent the beginning and the end of the same journey, and what Yeshua is simply and plainly stating to us is that "I am the Way." So it holds then that the gate which we leave through is also the portal of return.

Where the miracle plays its part is not at the Alpha or Omega points but the perceived distance between them. A careful look at the illustration should explain the effect more comprehensively.

A kind of an elliptical shape that is like an almost closed parabola exists between the Alpha and Omega points. Imagine this line of the elliptical shape divided up now into different segments. Imagine each and every one of the segments as a lifetime we scripted into our existence here on earth. As we progress on down this perceived parabolic path, some lifetime lessons can be dropped or skipped over, ultimately causing this ellipse or oval to shrink. How? We may well ask! This can be done by simply passing by everything that seems to irk us and by showing true forgiveness for all our brothers and sisters. Yeshua said it succinctly in two words.

"Be passersby."

And it can be seen in logion 42 of the apocryphal Saint Thomas Gospel. What Yeshua meant was to not let the day-to-day, endless distractions sidetrack us from why we are here and to acknowledge illusion for what it really is.

This is our spiritual prescription, for every single thing that comes our way has a distinct and definite reason for being there in the first place but only in the form of a lesson. Remember that there is nothing really out there, only disguised opportunities for love and forgiveness, and what are they but our master key to everyone's salvation. *A Course in Miracles* states:

"When you want only love you will see nothing else. Love, too, is recognized by its messengers. If you make love manifest, its messengers will come to you because you invited them."

So the effect of love and forgiveness on this, our imagined elliptical extension, is that by its length being reduced, we cancel out the segments where a lesson need not be learned. That has the stupendous effect of shortening the ellipse or oval, and that, my dear readers, that is a Miracle! Why? Because it means that we are now shortening all our perceived existences on this "nutso" planet earth; the dense smoke begins to lighten and dissipate; the mirrors once grimy and stained are becoming more and more translucent, transparent, and finally clear. Before the Infiniteness of Love's Light, we stand immaculate and innocent, holding the sight within our grasp of the Promise of Eternal Day, the promise of our Own True Reality, and this can only be by the Grace and Generosity of our Father's Love!

So you see that we have control over our lives even though they have probably been scripted with goodly input from ourselves, but does control of a dream really mean anything to us or does it even matter? Rather, we should excise and transcend the offending nature of this world and prepare for our return home.

We can delay this return indefinitely, but why would we even want to consider that for even the slightest moment? After all, if we delay it, we still have to live the lives we scripted without any element of change. But the idea of going home soon in a couple of short lifetimes with just a little forgiveness as opposed to, for instance, the incalculable horrors of a thousand or more lives, interspersed over a possible fifty thousand years, is a good enough reason to listen for the Call Home.

Raymond Pratt
Iuil 2006

Chapter 16
A God of Fear and the Notion of Hell

No matter what is taught to people at any given time, it is hard to dismantle certain preconceptions that have arisen throughout their experiences of life. One of the major preconceptions we have engrained within our faulty mind-set is the idea that God must be loved AND feared. The loving part, we can accept and understand well enough, but what about the fear aspect?

In the Catholic catechism there is a description of the Holy Spirit's gifts given to us. If I remember correctly they are:

Wisdom
Understanding
Council
Fortitude
Knowledge
Piety
and Fear of the Lord

Fear of the Lord? Pray tell me now, how can this be a gift? There is no wisdom that I can think of that can be gleaned from it, and there can hardly be any knowledge or piety in fear. I would never, ever dream of attempting to counsel anyone in the necessity of fear, for accepting it makes it real. So if these seven gifts of the Holy Spirit are considered true, then every one of the first six gifts given must become undone by the seventh. And in all honesty, the gift of fear has to be completely bogus, for it is no gift at all to anyone and it is only by the Holy Spirit's actions that all fear is tackled, released, and neutralized.

Why do we have to have this need to fear our own Loving Father, the one Holy All-Embracing Person who created us out of His extending Himself?

We were not created out of the dust or anything physically special, at least with regard to the spiritual part that makes us incredibly unique in the Eyes of God; we were truly created out of the continuous expansion of Pure Love in action. If there is anyone in this whole wide world that we would have a need to trust for any reason, it would have to be Him Alone.

And if our Father Himself is not trustworthy, then tell me who is? For if He is not the one to share the whole burden with, then there cannot be a God, because there is no one I know that could wear His Mantle!

You cannot have a God of Love and a God of Fear in the same person, it is impossible. Either He is one or the other, for a God of Love cannot understand fear and thus will not embrace it, because it is not of His making. Nor can a God of Fear, who deems it necessary to create a fortification to defend or attack, extend love, for both defense and attack only exist as an extension of fear.

Love is the absence of fear and guilt in a mind, and so it must follow, then, that fear must be the absence of love. So when we fail to love, we are only endorsing the element of fear. It is indeed impossible for both love and its opposite, fear, to be correct. So one of these has to be the creation of God, and the other must then exist as the creation of ego and us, ourselves, through our long, unnecessary association with ego's shenanigans. So it really doesn't strain the imagination a great deal or take too much to recognize who created what.

The fearful mind is one that we need to be vigilant against, for its misconceptions project from a mind that can only be at war with itself. A mind at war with itself cannot convey or project any sense of peace because peace is not a logical extension of fear. In our favorite book, *A Course in Miracles*, it states quite plainly that 'the whole notion of war deprives us of peace."

It is for this reason that a mind at peace cannot have both love and fear in it, as we cannot be awake and dreaming at the same time, and we cannot be serving two masters. If both try to cohabit in the mind at the same time, we will not be able to recognize anything of importance. This would include that ability to share the pure Love emanating from the Higher Mind of our own Mentor, the Holy Spirit.

Fear, in many ways, is correctly seen frequently as the reaction of a mind out of control. It cannot maintain its proper function within the higher mind of Spirit for it sees a need to counterattack or defend against what it incorrectly perceives. For this reason, it is very important to eliminate the false idea of fear and guilt from the Holy Spirit's agenda, for He only exists out of the extension of God's Love.

How the Catholic Church came to name the seven gifts of the Holy Spirit that I have previously mentioned is peculiar at best. If one takes a look in the Bible, there is a list of the Holy Spirit's gifts to us, and they don't really compare. The gifts shown are:

Meekness
Grace
Faith
Generosity
Self-Control
Long-Suffering
Peace Joy and Love

This, to me, feels much more like what the Holy Spirit is about, and not one of His nine gifts shown here could be listed as manipulative or thought-provoking.

However, I can gladly say that I see no mention of the need to have any "Fear of the Lord." I do not know, so I cannot say if the previous seven gifts shown that were suggested had an ulterior motive in hand but I will refrain from any other unnecessary comment. One can access the actual list showing the nine gifts of the Holy Spirit in the New Testament of any Christian Bible. It is located in Galatians 5:22-23.

The idea of a God of Fear is a notion created solely by man to manipulate his fellow man with the threat of exclusion to what is his "natural birthright." That we can nurture the mad idea of excluding our brother from his Father is most certainly not correct thinking and is an affront to man's Creator, God Himself. Such notions in themselves can truly be considered as being a strong case of blasphemy against Our Father in Heaven and His Creations, for they were all created equal together and all at the same time. And as we have always tried to stress, within our brothers and sisters lie those keys to our own salvation.

Likewise, the whole notion of Hell is not of God's understanding or creation. God sees absolutely no need for any other place but the Homeland He created for His errant souls, who left Him to be here in exile. But exile is a temporary place until we find ourselves and our Way home. If Heaven is the abode of our God of Love then Hell must be the abode of the God of Fear. It can only stand, then, that a prayer to a God of Fear cannot be a prayer at all, for it cannot be going to Heaven, and is this not where we wished to send it in the first place? If that is the case, all of our prayers made to a God of Fear that we feel we need to believe in must be going straight to Hell, for this is the domain of a God of Fear. So now, we must ask ourselves in all honesty, who and where are our thoughts and prayers directed to?

Hell is the domain of fear made incarnate, and it was most certainly created by ego and ourselves, for it does not exist as some dense, sulfurous lower astral plane. It exists here on earth, a place we created along with ego as our co-builder. Why would God have a need to create a Hell for us when we have made for ourselves a perfectly good representation of it here? But Hell is a very strange manifestation of our own sick, split minds that are in constant need of healing. The healing is there and available on request, that is, provided we access the right Physician.

What kind of a mind can indulge in the picture of seeing a brother trapped for ETERNITY in a fiery pit, surrounded by the provocations of screaming demons? Should we think that this is the one and only correct place for one of God's lost sparks? Because if we do entertain such a vile notion, we are then as mad as the proverbial hatter. We are indeed totally insane and our salvation is temporarily stymied. There is no way that our Father, our own Parent, would countenance such a scenario with his beloved son. But man often, in fact all too frequently, thinks he knows better!

Man is dualistic in nature and has always tried to influence different situations when there is a need to accomplish what he thinks is his own heart's desire. For instance, how many wars have we engaged in and unnecessarily fought, all to what end? And to what degree man can influence depends on the depth of his madness. On many occasions, he will conclude that his own cause is whole-heartedly justified and that "the end always justifies the means." Even if this means that he is going to be that Mr. Nice Guy for one minute and the Antichrist a short time later. Supposedly, this is our element of "love" and fear together in action, but they cannot exist, for the "love" shown is conditional and not real love at all! It is in every way a sham that can be seen for what it's worth.

When the idea of Hell was instigated by the early Christian Church, it had been under serious attack for a great many years. There were the persecutions, at first from the corrupt Roman emperors; then there were the competing religions, of which there were a great many. And then there was always the Gnostic way of thought and freethinkers to contend with, which saw the idea of massive organization as anathema in their search for God. So for the sake of commonality, the Church failed to entertain any flexibility in its rigid belief system that then ultimately eroded into theological dogma and the threat of Hell.

The idea of Hell was a relatively new one, and it did not correspond to the old Judaic version known as "Sheol," or even Gehenna, the pit that was probably what Yeshua was led to believe in during His Own religious upbringing. Sheol, to the Jews, was a kind of Hades, like in the Orpheus and Persephone tradition, a gray place for mortals, good, bad, and indifferent. And Gehenna was the pit where the trash was burned.

Readers, there can only be a God of Love. There is no God of Fear, and by logical extension, there cannot be a place called Hell. Unless man has decided that the place we inhabit right now is too good for some. He then may see a need to conjure up a lower echelon of Hell and torture for his brother. A man who can do this to a brother is insane, and will remain the sole denizen of his own nightmare.

Raymond Pratt
Deireadh Fomhair 2006

Chapter 17
Salvation Through Crucifixion or Resurrection

It was a very sad procession that made its way along the cobblestone path north from the Antonine fort toward the northern city gates at Sha'ar Shechem (the Sechem or Nablus or the Damascus Gate). This April weather should promise again, as was usually the case, what it generally delivered at the 2,500-foot elevation, moderately cool nights and quickly warming days. The whole painful, heartrending journey would be fairly short to this well-recognized site, it being the regular place of execution for some time now.

The Roman legions, with this now (probably) being the year 30 C.E., had been Jerusalem's and Israel's most determined, ruthless, hated, and unforgiving conquerors for well nigh on three generations. They indeed were very willing and quite adept in perfecting the ways and means of disposing of any perceived threats to their vast empire.

Yeshua had been preaching His unique and unusual message of hope and love to both the Jews and gentiles alike for anything from one to three years. He was well-known to the Jewish religious authorities and also to the ever present Roman occupiers, who had their own reasons to keep an eye on Him. The Romans were well versed in what could and did happen regularly during some of the major Jewish holidays. Yeshua had also been branded by all as a potential troublemaker. Nevertheless, by spending most of His Ministry in Galilee, He managed to keep out of Jerusalem's limelight.

There would always be a strong, unquenchable, and continuous desire for the long-awaited appearance of the coming Messiah (Hebrew: HaMesiach). This would remain as a core belief of the people's hearts, giving a constant and indomitable yearning to the long awaiting Children of Israel.

The place of execution outside the gates was known as Golgotha, or the Place of the Skull. This most probably referred to the reasonably-sized hill north of the city walls where the whole eroded western side bears a grim but very uncanny resemblance to the top part of a human skull, eye sockets included. It is also well documented to be a place of execution during the 500 long years of misrule of the Turkish Ottoman Empire. This very noticeable and large peculiarly created outcrop lay pretty much at the northern junction of the Jaffa, Jericho and Sechem (or Nablus) main roads. It also joined with the main arterial approach to the northern entrance of the city of Jerusalem.

Even up to about 200 years ago, executing criminals at certain crossroads seemed to be a distasteful but fairly prevalent judicial arrangement, particularly in the distant British Isles. The islands had been partially conquered and ruled by the Roman Empire for well over 400 years (with the sole exception of Hibernia, the island of Ireland and upper Caledonia, the northern part of Scotland). Many of the hauntings and terrors associated with the gibbet cross, that is, the crossroad locations where people were hung, are fairly well remembered. They would always remain a "bete noire" in people's memories even up to today, where they are not particularly occasioned by anyone on their night-time wanderings.

On our recent trip outside the city walls to the Garden Tomb (Hebrew: Gan HaKever) located beside Golgotha, my mother and I completed a number of visits. The site is not very well known to its Christian visitors. Nevertheless, we came to the conclusion that this rather secluded spot felt much more like the place of Resurrection than the Church of the Holy Sepulcher within the city walls. It would seem that the Holy Sepulcher has been owned by six Christian churches. These same six churches still see an ongoing need to squabble ferociously over confusingly ancient rights and privileges. To compound this not so little matter further, the key-holder happens to be, and must be by law, a Muslim.

One can now view the approximate place of Yeshua's execution and Resurrection close to the Garden Tomb, which is well run by a very helpful, friendly, and non-denominational British group.

This execution place was not located on the hill but beside and at the bottom of it. The hill to the east is much higher than those previously imagined in many of the Renaissance paintings of the Crucifixion. However, the whole Garden Tomb area does exude such peace and tranquility that it makes all visits to this location a heartfelt joy. It must remind us of some kind of Remembrance of God, for I felt no sense of misfortune here. The old execution area close by, on the other hand, exudes no such peace and now contains the central hub of the Palestinian bus system. They operate solely in the West Bank and East Jerusalem or Al Quds (The Holy) as the city is simply known in Arabic.

THE TWO POSSIBLE PLACES OF EXECUTION

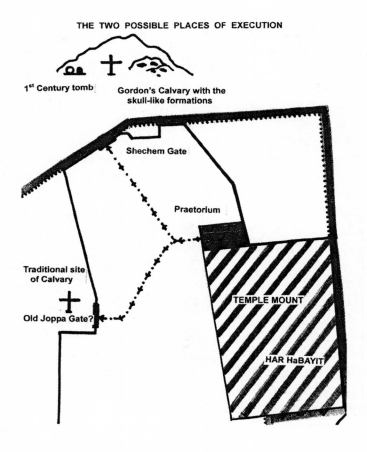

1st Century tomb

Gordon's Calvary with the skull-like formations

Shechem Gate

Praetorium

Traditional site of Calvary

Old Joppa Gate?

TEMPLE MOUNT

HAR HaBAYIT

Our question that we now have to ask ourselves is whether man was saved by Yeshua's Crucifixion, or by His Resurrection. Or was he saved possibly by both, or could there really be a genuine need for all this to happen in the first place? Was Yeshua's Blood necessary to be spilt and His short life unsparingly taken for our Salvation?

Here again the whole necessity of spilling blood rears its large ugly head. What is it with human beings that they regard this sick and unnatural compunction to sacrifice some physical part of themselves, and use it over and over as a tool simply to find salvation? Salvation means to be "saved from" and what is it that we need to be saved from? Salvation implies that we are lost and can't find our way but that is not, nor ever has been, the case. Our home in Heaven is forever guaranteed for it is part of our divine birthright, just like the Prodigal Son who could never be wrong under any circumstances in his Father's Loving eyes.

Some are envisioned with the idea of the "no pain, no gain" mentality. What reality, tell me, exists in this idea that blood must be spilled in copious amounts, ad nauseam, to "balance" the books? Whose books need to be balanced? Even the whole idea of "balance" and "adjustment" are pure and unadulterated duality, a faulty mind-set that tends to be so pernicious and devastating to our correct Vision. What we need to staunch and stem immediately is the absolutely maddening flow of notions that some form of sacrifice is desperately needed. This is, again, taken from a complete misunderstanding of the Jewish scriptures. The whole idea comes directly, as usual, from the Old Testament and, as such, continues in earnest to harangue and haunt some of the mainstream Christian belief systems. This can only be a faulty and mistaken belief system where occasions for the spilling of blood are not only condoned but have been, up to the very recent past, regretfully, very heartily endorsed

.On the top of the Mount of Olives, and overlooking the eastern wall of the city, there used to be a sacrificial place. Incidentally this place was on or close to the high road to the village of Bethany (Hebrew, Beit Ani for poor house). Bethany was one of the dormitory villages that lay close to Jerusalem and was frequently used by Yeshua during His latter days, as Martha, Mary, and Lazarus lived there. It is nowadays an old Arab village called Al Azzariya, and thus named after Lazarus.

The sacrificial place on top of the Mount of Olives was used for the killing and burning of the "Red Heifer," where the priests covered themselves with its ashes as a symbol of salvation. This would be another symbol taken up by the early Christian Church, for on Palm Sunday, Yeshua, on His way to Jerusalem, passed by or fairly close to this same spot coming from Bethany. The idea presented to us is that Yeshua is now to be seen as the "the new sacrifice." *A Course in Miracles* states in the chapter, "The Guilt-less Son of God" page 240, about the Crucifixion being the symbol of ego:

> "When ego was confronted with the real guiltlessness of God's Son it did attempt to kill Him, and the reason it gave was that guiltlessness is blasphemous to God. To the ego, the ego is God, and guiltlessness must be interpreted as the final guilt that fully justifies murder."

Yeshua could not and did not die for our sins! Why would He, for there was no need, as there were no sins to die for. He was always able to see the Father's Work and Glory shining through the illusory bodies of His brothers. He saw their innocence, their frailty and their wanderlust; but he also blessed the wonder of His Father in them. After all, did He not see Himself as their Shepherd?

The idea of salvation through pain and death on the Cross is totally foreign to corrected thinking. It places an emphasis on the express need for all bodies to suffer. If Yeshua was indeed meant to suffer for our "sins," this, in effect, would create such tremendous guilt. And tell me, why would He consider doing such a thing, when all His teachings intimated the opposite?

Yeshua overcame death on that "sad" day just to show us how unimportant the body is, NOT how holy it could be, and that we should try to effect those same results as well. He wanted to show us His Victory over the deepest depths of human misery and how our common soul is able to soar above all. Nowadays, we try to emphasize the grim illusory thought of Yeshua's death, and it is at the sole expense of the Infinite Reality He returned to. This Reality in question, however, was never, ever in doubt for any of His brothers. The Innocent can only know innocence; the "guilty" must simply forgive!

We are perfect creations of the Father and believe it or not, if we wish, we are totally innocent, always have been that way, and always will be! To think of our innocence and guiltlessness as blasphemous is how ego wants us to see its world, for it would have murdered the Son of God if it had been able to.

Yes, Yeshua was indeed crucified most horribly, but it was His Resurrection that became our new shining beacon and signposted route home to the Father. Until we are able to understand, accept, and proclaim our innocence of His Crucifixion, which seems so nonexistent in us, we will still believe that we are guilty, and will we not continue to find a way to blame ourselves? And indeed if this is going to be the case, will we then not endeavor to blame our brothers also for His death on the Cross? But all this projected guilt on our brother is only a thorn in our own brow, a nail in our hand, and a lance in our side.

Think about it well! The man out there who wishes to believe in salvation through pain and sacrifice is in serious error. Why? Because he sees the need for a brother, and himself also, to suffer continuously and needlessly, all but for a chance sniff at salvation.

Are we so forgiving in our own agendas to be in such a position to effectively comprehend the profound needs of our brother, our Father's loving creation?

Salvation is everyone's birthright without question in the end, for it has always been our Loving Father's Sole Intention!

Raymond Pratt
Deireadh Fomhair 2006

Chapter 18
What is Sacred, Idols and the Altar of Form

Around 1500 B.C.E., the patriarch Abraham, Sarah, and their offspring lived with their extended nomadic family in the northern Negev region of southern Israel and Palestine. Between that time and the Exodus of the Israelites from the slavery of Egypt, Jerusalem, to the north, remained a small town occupied by a tribe known as the Jesubites. Abraham's families were concentrated between the towns of Hebron and Beersheva (Hebrew for seven wells), where water and ample grazing lands were readily available for the accompanying flocks and herds. It would take some years, roughly 500 of them in all, before a King David, around 1000 B.C.E., would build a small walled city just to the south of the present day Temple Mount (Hebrew is Har HaBayit) and a little east of Mount Zion (Hebrew is Har Tsiyyon). King Solomon, this well-known and resplendent heir and son of David, would build a brand-new temple to Yahweh and place their Holy Ark of the Covenant and contents within the inner sanctum or Holy of Holies of this great edifice.

Prior to the building of the new temple, the Holy Ark was kept in the care of the Levites, a priestly sect and one of the twelve tribes of Israel. The Ark was placed in a special guarded tent and contained within it, Aaron's staff, the Ten Commandments in stone, and the Urim and Thummim. These stones were very possibly the ancient stones of prophesy but all were considered sacred. After about forty years of wandering in the Sinai desert, a new generation of much less Egyptianized Israelites eventually managed to settle down in Judah. The Ark was then kept in the little hamlet of Kiryat Ye'arim (Hebrew for City of Trees?), at present, close to a small Arab town west of Jerusalem, hard by the West

Bank border called Abu Ghosh, and named after an eighteenth century sheikh.

Before this, the Philistines (Hebrew is Plishteem) had stolen the Ark when it had been ceremoniously but imprudently carried into battle to assure a victory that was, in actuality, a defeat. This spectacular loss to Israel was very short-lived for the Philistines gladly returned it after it was found it to be an increasingly major liability. So strong was the Philistine influence on the Israelite borderlands that more than a few of the Israelites clans still held on to old and questionable beliefs. They had to be dissuaded by their Prophet Samuel from their belief system and usage of the Philistine Baal and Asteroth statues found to be in their possession.

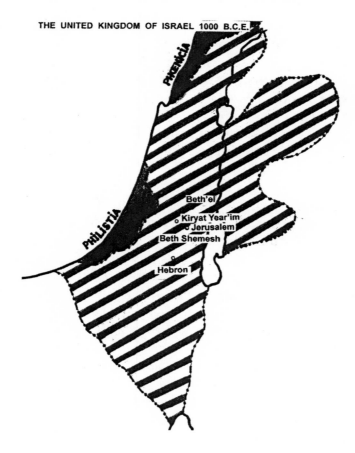

THE UNITED KINGDOM OF ISRAEL 1000 B.C.E.

The story of the Ark's subsequent removal to the city of Jerusalem by King David is to be found in the Bible's Old Testament in 1 Chronicles 13. It was moved to the capital approximately twenty years later.

Here you can see the Ark being used as a kind of idol and, most noticeably, a holy item by the standards of the day. The Ark remained in many places during its all too frequent wanderings, but does that make all of these places holy and sacrosanct? Joshua's field located in Beth Shemesh (Hebrew for the House of the Sun and originally called after a Canaanite sun god) where the cattle and cart stopped of its own while bringing back the Ark from the Philistines, was that holy?

Its next location in Kiryat Ye'arim, where it spent a brief time and for that matter, the Holy of Holies in the new Temple in Jerusalem, were both places considered to be holy by its being there also? Or did it then have to involve the ritualistic and sacrificial spilling of blood, by the rampant and unnecessary wholesale slaughter of animals on Temples' Mount Moriah to make it holy? Did all this need to occur in a "holy" place where Abraham intended to sacrifice his own son to his One God? Tell me in all honesty, what is so very sacred and holy about taking the life of your first-born?

Jerusalem of old has been conquered, pillaged, and destroyed many, many times and has seen the spillage of copious amounts of blood, all to what avail? It would be done by the Babylonians, the Assyrians, and by the Romans and the Persians, Crusaders, Mamelukes, and Islamic sultanates. In this most recent century, in 1947, the Jewish Quarter was completely destroyed by the Arab Legion army of the Hashemite kingdom of Jordan, during the bloody formation of the new Israel.

Jerusalem is considered a holy city by three major religions and is the center of the Jewish belief system. It is considered the possible pivotal location and worldly capital for the coming Jewish Messiah. Secondly it is well known for Yeshua's life, death, and Resurrection, and thirdly for Mohammad's night ride to heaven from the "levitating" stone in the center of the Dome of the Rock, the ornate Harem ash Sharif (Arabic for the Noble Sanctuary). In the famous Islamic book Umm Al-Kitab (Arabic for the Mother of

Books) held in Heaven as the Qu'ran tells us; all of us, Muslim, Christian, and Jew, are all considered to be the "Children of the Book." But even to this day at any given time, there still exists so much frustration between all of these three major religions, even in the Old City itself.

One can always judge the tree by the fruit it bears. We should find that the sole nature of this concept of holiness is indeed totally misplaced, jaundiced, highly suspect, and horrific!

If holiness can be judged and accorded such highly favored status by the amount of blood spilt over the past 3,500 years, there is a very good chance that the Old City of Jerusalem would win hands down! Otherwise there has to be something wrong-minded in the way that we and all religious groupings perceive holiness and what's sacred.

In every circumstance where we have perceived something as being holy or sacred, a number of issues have arisen:

1. What we have considered holy or sacred is perishable.
2. What we have considered holy or sacred was then created by man or nature.
3. What we have considered as our creation is man's representation of godliness and holiness and thus can only be an idol.
4. One man's idol is another man's anathema thus only creating a dualistic division and therefore must be a product of the nature of ego's realm.

So trying to understand holiness simply by man's considerations leaves a flaw due to the nature of how he perceives. Consider this situation for a moment. I am teaching a class of approximately thirty students. I now decide to pass around my favorite bag of hard minty humbug candies. By the time this bag comes back to me, I find that there is not a candy to be seen. I then suffer from loss, from deprivation, regret, and sorrow because I now have no candies left.

Now consider that I give a short class concerning, let's say, the nature of the Holy Spirit to all thirty pupils. Yes, I am sharing, but now on a completely different level, and it's not on the level of form; it's sharing on the level of Mind. Do I still suffer loss, deprivation, regret, etc. now? Not at all! Au contraire, my friend, I am making something that much bigger than it originally was, by the simple sharing of what I have at hand, in this case it would have to be, namely, Truth. Love is similar, but love on the level of form is totally conditional; for instance, if you don't love me, I won't love you and so such love dies, for there is nothing holy in place here.

Unconditional Love, on the other hand, is like what it says, unconditional, and because of its higher nature, it is of the Mind, is a constant and can only expand to become all-encompassing. This pertains to our holiness at work. Holiness can only come from one place, and it is not on the level of form or, if you wish, of this world. The holiness in us emanates solely from the Holy Trinity's correction process given to us and particularly from the Voice or Remembrance of God, or as we know Him, the Holy Spirit. We are all holy but, unfortunately, it all too often remains unrecognized.

A good and honest way to ascertain our personal connection with the Holy Spirit is to mull over this very simple little saying,

"How I see the world is a projection of how I am inside."

If we see the world as a dark, woe-begotten, and forbidding place filled with all kinds of undesirables, then it's probably time to reconsider our teacher. Could it be that it's ego teaching us, because it most certainly cannot be the Holy Spirit.

Look at Christianity with all its dogmas and idols, for example, transubstantiation, the blood of Yeshua, the Shroud of Turin, the Holy Grail, the Holy Cross, even the Immaculate Conception. Were all of these a necessity to initiate Yeshua's flowering, completing, and subsequent promotion of the "Good News" concerning the events and message of His brief existence here? In fact Yeshua never mentioned anything about these items. Why? Because they are all but a fabrication of the early Christian Church. In all honesty, much of this early Christian esoterica stems from, and was very probably fabricated in, those same early centuries with the added input of St. Helena of Byzantium in the fourth century. St. Helena incidentally was the mother of the Roman Empire's pagan

Emperor Constantine, the first ruler who supposedly embraced Christianity on his deathbed.

As for Yeshua, He cared not a jot for His Own body nor what happened to it. He was using it primarily as a means to explain to us that it should simply be seen for what it is, a vehicle for forgiveness to be transcended, and then left aside and forgotten.

Did it matter if Mary, His mother, was a virgin bride or for that matter, even married?

This idea stems from the Church's strange notion of "original sin," which we all are supposed to have been born with, with Mary being the sole exception. There is no original sin, only original innocence. Original sin is a human fabrication to simply place Mary one rung up the divine stepladder above us, in other words, a "special relationship." To believe in this as the sole truth would give so much credence to this whole silly, misguided idea of the sacredness of the body, a notion that does not and cannot exist at all. The body itself, together with the time and space it exists in, is only a tool to be used. It is there to be used to make the ultimate break with ego's hegemony here on its own turf. And it exists in helping to lift the veils of forgetfulness from our own true nature, by deep and pure forgiveness, but only with the help of the Right Teacher.

So how about the Holy Birthplace in Bethlehem? Should I mention that Galilee had a Bethlehem, too, and it was located fairly close to Nazareth, in the direction of Sepporis, the town where Mary was born? Bethlehem in Hebrew is "Beit Lehem," which means House of Bread, and how many of those can we imagine exist in Judea, Samaria, and in Galilee? Was it really holy or was it that Matthew, the local Gospel writer known to be of Jewish origin, was trying to make some kind of formal blood link of distinctiveness. A link mainly forged by the doubts, or necessity, between Yeshua and the royal house of David to give some semblance of credibility to His Jewish messianic destiny.

Would this make Yeshua a kind of Davidic blood heir and possible usurper in a sense to Herod's throne? The synoptic Gospel writers Mark and John are quiet and make no mention at all of such a birthplace.

There is absolutely nothing in the material world that is holy or sacred, for holiness and sanctity can only exist in the right Mind, and there is no Resurrection of the body for the Resurrection pertains only to the joined and healed Mind. And if the body is not of God's creation why would it return there?

So can there honestly be any real reason to drag some excuse for an aging, dilapidated, putrefying, and stinking electro-biological lump of protoplasm into the eternal antechamber of the Divine Presence? Absolutely not! It is but a faulty creation of the split mind syndrome that we have. It is especially well suited for the world it was adequately designed for, and by the dubious and highly unreliable agenda of that old shyster again, Dr. Ego.

What is of God's creation can only be eternal, and this being so, it must return to embrace Him. What is of man's creation is of a temporary nature and thus stays, if need be, to haunt him here where he created it.

We have to try and understand how to regain our connection with our higher Mind by first being aware of it. For the only result that can be ascertained of the body ruling the mind will be summed up in one familiar word, addiction, and addiction comes in many, many forms. There is the addiction of needing idols, the addiction of apathy, the addiction of holiness in its convoluted and "special relationship" sense. There is the addiction of fear and fearing God, the addiction of not wanting to know Truth, the addiction of ignorance being true bliss.

Yes, people feel comfortable in their addictions, and inertia is, in itself, a state of "gemutlichkeit" but we were given the tools to return to our Parent. Do we use them now or do we wait around again for another spin of the reincarnation roulette wheel?

The Second Coming will arrive for certain, but not heralded with a blast of celestial trumpets and a flaming sword as St. Paul would have us believe. It will arrive, and only when we have opened ourselves up to the One True Teacher that we will always have amongst us here. But that also means disregarding all the familiar idols we are innately accustomed to, our addictions, our fears, our petty machinations against our brothers and sisters. They are, have been, and can only be completely as innocent as we are. And yes indeed, we all are truly innocent, so to continue and progress effectively, we must endorse this notion well. This is our own spiritual "cold turkey" time!

Are miracles holy? They most certainly are because they are the creative results of the joining of Minds, and Minds joined are of the Kingdom of the Holy Spirit. The joining of Minds makes the need for any of our relevant projections void, for instance, fear, guilt, and sickness are unnecessary so they can and do on many occasions simply disappear. This is done efficaciously when we forgive our brother, for when we forgive our brother we forgive ourselves. When we forgive ourselves, we can then see ourselves as completely innocent. The Father has always known this but we don't know it. At least we don't know, not until we are in unison with our Higher Mind and have renewed our Remembrance of God our Parent, for innocents are what we intrinsically are.

The Recognition of "Innocence" and Guiltlessness is a major part of our Memory of God. If we can remember it, then one of the veils has been recognized and thus can acted upon and lifted.

Our now familiar book, *A Course in Miracles*, has this to say:

"The ego is trying to teach you how to gain the whole world and lose your own soul. The Holy Spirit teaches that you cannot lose your soul and there is no gain in the world, for of itself it profits nothing. To invest without profit is surely to impoverish yourself, and the overhead is high. Not only is there no profit in the investment but the cost to you is enormous."

The *Course* goes on to say that the acceptance of the world's reality will cost you your own Reality. God's Reality is sacred, but ego's reality of the mundane world can only be profane. Ego's rule in this world of form is provisional and can be summed up in one sentence;

"Seek and do not find."

We make elaborate altars to many forms, and all of these forms are idols that will have to be, sooner or later, replaced. These altars can only honor the fading glories and trivial triumphs of ego and its realm. These altars commemorate ancient and long forgotten victories over us. So why on earth would we want to praise and glorify this hard and vicious taskmaster who tries to keep us continually in chains?

It must be another unchecked addiction of some kind, not readily recognized. For we must have allowed ourselves to consider, avail, and peruse this addiction, but all it is doing is delaying our eventual Exodus.

"In perfect peace Yeshua waits for you at His Father's altar, holding out the Father's Love to you in the quiet light of the Holy Spirit's blessing. At the altar of God, the holy perception of God's Son becomes so enlightened that light streams into it, and the spirit of God's Son shines in the Mind of the Father and becomes one with it." (From *A Course in Miracles*)

Take a close look at Ego's altar. It's old, stained, and decrepit; it is not a new altar by any means but one left behind and standing from the dawn of man's "mistake" a long, long time ago. It still stands and will continue to do so due to our own listless apathy and our mental and spiritual inertia. Because of this, we are falsely led to feel it's convenient, understandable, and that we must be comfortable with it.

If we listen awhile we just might hear a Whisper in the Wind. Is it calling us by our name, like some ancient, vaguely remembered nickname from our youth half forgotten? Or is it perhaps like a brisk and freshening breeze disturbing some cobwebbed window hangings of antiquity, all slowly deteriorating in the den of a stuffy airless back room? That Whisper is now plainly calling us to build our new Altar, our new Temple in the midst of our healing Mind. There is no mighty call for forgiveness through pain and guilt, nor is there any kind of sacrifice needed, no blood-letting, no complicated or special, elaborate prayers. There is only the incessant and anxious Call of our own Parent beside us trying to wake us up from this torturing and tempestuous dream world that we have decided to call life!

Raymond Pratt
Lunasa 2006

JERUSALEM'S RELIGIOUS QUARTERS AS OF NOW

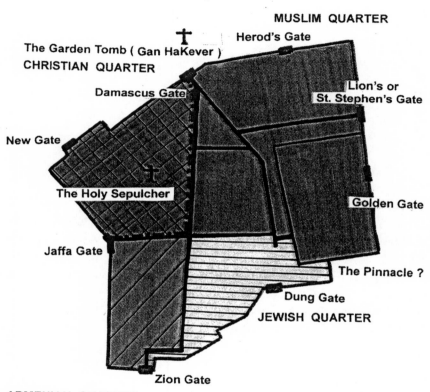

MUSLIM QUARTER

Herod's Gate

The Garden Tomb (Gan HaKever)
CHRISTIAN QUARTER

Lion's or
St. Stephen's Gate

Damascus Gate

New Gate

The Holy Sepulcher

Golden Gate

Jaffa Gate

The Pinnacle ?

Dung Gate

JEWISH QUARTER

Zion Gate

ARMENIAN QUARTER

Chapter 19
The Holy Land Journal + May 2006

A few weeks after arriving back in the United States from my very first trip to the Holy Land, I decided to call my mother, who lives in Ireland. She had always shown considerable interest in a possible visit to the old city of Jerusalem and now, it was all up to me to convince her that it was a feasible proposition and quite safe.

I think she had some misgivings, but that changed as I told her of what I had seen prior. I had seen her, all in my mind's eye, sitting in a metallic-colored car, gold or silver, and together, the two of us driving into the hills toward Jerusalem. I also told her that I saw her flying to or from Tel Aviv in a dark gray or black two-piece suit as I could picture myself onboard with some effort, climbing over her sleeping presence quietly while en route to Israel and the rear washroom.

A few months later and we are on our way. We were to fly from Dublin to Paris on Cityjet, change planes and take ELAL to Tel Aviv, arriving fairly early in the morning. The layover would be about six hours in Paris. I found that the airport in Paris's Charles De Gaulle was just about as uninteresting as the one I found in Frankfurt-am-Main the previous February. But some of the staff proved this time to be a good deal less friendly. ELAL, the principal Israeli airline, had changed their two flights that evening to only one. To accommodate all of the passengers, they brought in a large Boeing 747-400 jumbo jet, one I was acquainted with, which I knew would probably shorten the journey by around forty-five minutes, more or less. Great, I thought, as I was now by this time, pretty well tired after traveling all of the previous day from Salt Lake City to Dublin.

However, the ELAL airline security people in Paris were unhelpful. In all honesty, it sounded and really felt like they were trying to indirectly manipulate my mother into saying things, who knows, something detrimental about me, and most probably herself as well. But this kind of really primitive psychological tactic, (give 'em enough rope) no matter how especially obnoxious and superficial that it seemed, didn't and couldn't work and so we boarded the flight for the uneventful journey.

Arriving very early the next morning in Ben Gurion airport, the car we rented was upgraded automatically to a silver Mazda 3. We drove into the eastern hills only to get caught in the early morning incoming Jerusalem traffic. I parked in a small Palestinian parking lot outside and quite close to the north side Damascus Gate, whose sole attendant proceeded to offer me a real good rate. The unfortunate thing was that I had to make two trips, schlepping all the bags back uphill to the now familiar Casa Nova hotel where parking places just do not exist. Mother decided to take it easy for the rest of the day by exploring the quaint stores and having a look around in the Christian Quarter and Jaffa Gate. An attempt at the Holy Sepulcher would be tried in the morning.

In the days of long ago when they said, "I'm going up to Jerusalem!" they really meant what they said. The city is ALL hills and outside of the walls it is even worse. The hills would ultimately affect my mother's enjoyment of the city, whose ups and downs used to be a good deal higher and deeper. In fact, both the Kidron and Hinnom valleys to the east and west used to be at least fifty feet deeper in places. The combined debris, however, of the 2,000 years of constant warfare, rebuilding, earthquakes, and natural accumulation has filled them in. There once was a time when the city needed an effective bridge to cross from the Mount of Olives to the city and Temple Mount. This was most probably a very similar bridge that stood in this place when Yeshua crossed over the Kidron Valley on that fateful Palm Sunday but has by now long disappeared.

Mother took a quick visit to the Church of the Holy Sepulcher the following day, and she came out with a bad taste in her mouth. There had been large crowds, mostly Romanians, and one of the black-clad Greek Orthodox priests was initiating some kind of selective crowd control while also taking money handouts from the

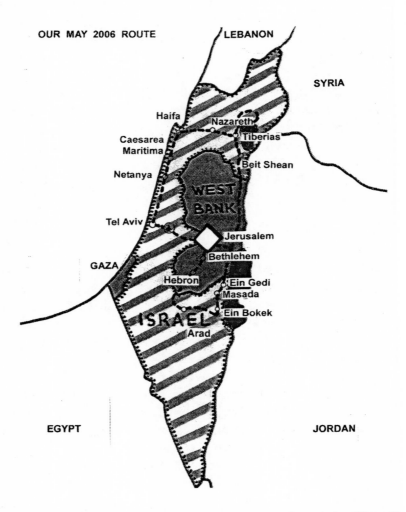

visiting faithful. It did not seem to be the correct time or place to be doing this, but it was a fait accompli. He would then slip the money into one of his pockets while trying to offer some token resemblance of fairness and order to the waiting lines.

As I have mentioned before, I have never found the Holy Sepulcher to be one of my favorite sites. It is one I give a wide berth to. The one site that my mother loved was the Garden Tomb (Hebrew: Gan HaKever) and it was situated not so very far from the Damascus Gate.

Before going there, however, we went shopping in the Cardo, the old, partly restored Roman throughway excavated in the Jewish Quarter. To walk to the Garden Tomb the shortest way is directly through the Muslim Quarter where I would pass by the old Hashimi hostel where I stayed that February prior. On our traipse down the Suq Khan ez-Zeit street, a young Palestinian adult man with a homemade cart brimming with rather large and heavy wooden planks bumped both purposely and most unnecessarily into my mother. I was shocked and immediately grabbed hold of the cart and pushed aside his protruding planks, almost toppling them and the cart over while shouting at the man for his complete lack of concern. This would raise an instant hubbub with the local Muslim shopkeepers on the street, who were quick to admonish the offending cart-pusher and were most apologetic to us. The whole incident honestly could not have lasted more than probably twenty seconds, but it did put a damper on the rest of the day's activities.

The Gan HaKever, or the Garden Tomb if you wish, proved to be my mother's favorite place in Jerusalem. It was a tranquil spot and exuded an engagingly profound sense of peace not readily available within the walls of the old city. It is a place where you can relax and reclaim a good deal of your composure, something we really needed to do after our very brief interlude in the Muslim Quarter's alleys. It is most fortunate, too, in a sense, that the Garden Tomb's location is not readily recognized by many of the Christian churches as a valid contestable location. As such, it was therefore not too inclined to be overrun by springtime tourists. It is, however, still very popular with some Protestant denominations. But in all honesty, it should not matter at all as to where Yeshua arose, but I would like to think that it might have been done from such an enchanting spot as this.

The next day while visiting bookshops in the Jaffa Gate area, we were approached by "John." John wanted to show us Bethlehem in his private car for a substantial fee. He stated that he was a Maronite Christian, but I had my doubts about that. He drove us quickly through the West Bank checkpoint area, and in a short while we were in Manger Square where the famous Holy Church of the Nativity is situated.

John handed us over to the local Muslim church guide holding a Palestinian permit, who was rather nice, and he gave us a good tour. We tipped him handsomely and later were brought to a store selling expensive bric-a-brac. It was obvious to me there must have been some kind of shenanigans going on between John, the guide, and the storekeeper. But we didn't mind too much as we sincerely thought that we would be helping the ailing Palestinian economy. While we were traveling in the Holy Land, the Israelis had begun to impose a ban on fuel products entering the West Bank. We thought that this would have a most detrimental effect, for it was the result of the Hamas party having won the Palestinian election. Hamas does not believe that Israel should exist and will not deal with any of the Israeli authorities. And so everything then ends up back at square one again as seems to always be the case.

The next day we headed off down the road toward the Dead Sea. We passed by the small oasis of En Gedi and stopped by the Masada Rock; however, Mom did not want to take the cable car to the top, and the walk was a little steep. We continued on to the little seaside tourist town of En Bokek and went down to the salty blue sea to wet our toes. All of the people there on the beach, and there were quite a few, tended to be a very friendly, sociable, and a most engaging bunch. We continued on our drive toward Arad, a newish town above the Dead Sea and to the west that had a rather new spartan look to it. Continuing west for a little while, we then started to head back north toward Hebron, on our way back home to Jerusalem.

At the West Bank border we picked up some rather surly Israeli settlers who were trying to hitch-hike home and who lived close to Hebron in a compound in Kiryat Arba. Remember that Hebron is the very old city where it all started in the beginning, with the patriarch Abraham and his sons Isaac and Ishmael. The Israelite nation is considered to be the sole descendents of Isaac (Yitzak meaning "he laughs"), Abraham and Sarai's progeny. The Arab nations were, in turn, supposedly, to have been considered the sole descendents of Abraham's first son, through Hagar, and he was called Ishmael (Ishma'el meaning God hears). But they were certainly both sons of Abraham, not that you would think it now from the way their descendents treat each other. I would also like to consider this whole affair between these brothers as what one would envision a private family matter. This is effectively two sons arguing over old land and boundary lines that their own father left them. It is unfortunate that these new Israeli settlers seem to be more than just a little hostile toward their local Arab brothers, but Mother, the settlers, and I went ahead and got home safely.

The following day we left Jerusalem to drive up the Jordan Valley to view the beautiful Sea of Galilee and its surrounding mountains. This was Yeshua's home turf. We stopped occasionally for gas wherever we could see a station but one has to be quite alert for the word "gas" written in the unique Hebraic letters, which are GZ in their local language. As we approached Beit She'an, a small city at the north end of the Jordan Valley, we went into a little mall to eat some fast food and try to change some dollars into shekels. It sounds like a pretty simple affair but oh, no! my Hebrew was just not that proficient enough for this kind of situation, and their English was a whole lot worse. So we made the complete transaction, funnily enough, in French. Yes, a stray Irishman in Israel changing American money in French!

A half an hour later we arrived in the main town of Tiberias and we found another Casa Nova almost right beside the Sea of Galilee. They only charged us $35 per night per room all inclusive with good air conditioning, a shower, and a decent Israeli breakfast thrown in for good measure.

That very evening we went around the corner of our hotel to eat at a lakeside restaurant known to specialize in St. Peter's fish. The fish is a kind of tilapia indigenous to the lake and naturally would be associated with the Apostle's namesake. As we took our lakeside seats by a table, we were soon accosted by a substantial number of sparse-haired felines who, I suppose, were also quite partial to St. Peter's fish. Omar, our Palestinian waiter, then threw some stale pita bread into the lake, and almost immediately, several huge catfish appeared and wolfed the lot down. The peculiar way the cats balanced themselves on the boardwalk's edge, with total and complete abandon to their potential predicament, was entertaining. I then idly wondered whether they had occasionally toppled into the lake to give such massive catfish as these their name. The meal was wonderful as was the scenery superb and what we did not finish, the local performing cats did consume with great gusto. As we headed slowly back toward our lodgings that were close by, we saw a disco boat pull out from the lake dock. This is surely an Israeli invention of sorts that tries to keep their young, healthy teenagers occupied and amused for a few hours in a relatively safe place.

Mother did like Tiberias (Hebrew is Tveriyya) with its friendly people. I also became very fond of the place. The following day we went to the Caparnaum area where Yeshua preached. We visited Magdala and stopped at Tabgtha (Heptapegon in Greek for the seven springs), where one of the Miracle of the Loaves and Fishes was accomplished. We drove by the old ruins of the town of Chorazim mentioned by Yeshua for their lack of faith. It is hard not to fall in love with Galilee's beautiful scenery (the Hebrew for it is HaGalil HaGoyim, the District of the Foreigners, and it probably pertains to the Babylonian Jews who returned here) and I went so far as to promise myself another visit to Northern Israel.

Our next day was spent preparing to go back to the USA but first with a short stop in Nazareth on our drive back to the airport outside Tel Aviv. Nazareth is a mostly Christian Arab town and the largest in Galilee. It is about two-thirds Christian in its religious makeup and, as one can imagine, one-third Muslim also. Most of the minority Jewish population who live locally tend to live together in Nazareth Illit (Hebrew for Upper Nazereth), close by in the surrounding hills. I found it, at first, very hard to navigate through the narrow winding streets that were in general, insufficiently signposted. After a short while of searching we found our way back on to the Haifa road.

Haifa is Israel's third largest city and continues to be the main port and was repeatedly hit by many of the rockets fired from the Hezbollah positions in Lebanon this year (2006). It also happens to be the main spiritual center for the Baha'i believers, who own a very graceful and domed building situated in very beautiful stepped gardens, all overlooking the city and the bay. It is also the locale for the minority but secretive Druze Faith, who live in the Mount Carmel area here. We could not spend enough time to see all here in Haifa but continued on for about eight miles past and took a break.

One of the things I like about Israel is that it is not overloaded with stupid and well-scoffed bylaws. I was never stopped at any time, ever, by the prevalent police presence, and the young army conscripts were, all in all, educated and friendly. After passing Haifa's port on the Number Two Interstate we pulled over onto the hard shoulder and then onto the soft shoulder, parked, and walked down to the beach. No one gave us any grief about parking, and it was nice to get some quiet beach time before leaving to go home.

At the airport while checking in, I found that I had left my camera in the rented car. An hour later, I had the missing camera in my hands as we began to board our ELAL night flight for New York.

After arriving in New York, everything went wrong. We went to the Delta terminal only to find that it was closed and had been moved to another terminal. Then the flight we were supposed to take was cancelled. Fortunately I had some tickets for Jetblue Airways also, but via the Denver airport and that flight was delayed en route because of the weather and a possible medical emergency landing. Fortunately we did not have to make any emergency landing and later that day we arrived in Salt Lake City, completely disheveled and then only to find all our bags missing but for an hour. Continuing along our way home to Stansbury Park, I got a flat, ten miles from anywhere, and naturally found my tire iron to be missing. We would then end up waiting a whole hour and a half for help on the very busy Interstate 80 as my cell phone, now by this time, was dead. But help would arrive eventually for it always does.

It is so "nice" to arrive back home exhausted from a long extended trip straight into the hands of a major ego attack and that's what it exactly was! This was, for me, proof positive that we always need to be vigilant against ego for it likes to catch us off balance.However, the Holy Land was an experience that we both enjoyed and one that Mother would always have in her mind to remember for the rest of her life.

Raymond Pratt
Eanair 2007

Chapter 20
Sexuality & How It Divides Us

Sexuality, hmmm! You did not honestly think that I would have to drag this subject into the open light to discuss in lurid detail, did you? However, it does in itself play a particularly potent role, whose ramifications can have within it powerful lessons in love and forgiveness. Wherever we proceed, sexuality has to, it seems, not only endow us with ego's ingrained guilt factor but also with its continual and ubiquitous nature. It constantly seems to regale in our face pretty much on every single day of our existence. This then being the case, honest readers, it tends to make sexuality one of a number of superior lynchpins that ego deftly uses to reinforce our perceived exile. For the uninitiated among us, it is truly the vain and inglorious personification of our division and our dualistic nature.

In the world of spirit we are all one, but here in this world of form we are unknowingly dissociated from the Oneness by the "need" to be separate and independent. When I say unknowingly, I mean that when the decision was made by us to abandon our eternal home, a veil of forgetfulness descended upon us to hide the truth. We then became fearful, and built our fortifications against an enemy who was really ourselves in disguise. These over utilized ramparts that we continue to build around ourselves only serve ego by enhancing our aloofness from our brothers all around us. The results must only then reflect a world of hostile borders, and the inherent tension they ultimately bring. The very same idea that we are trying to expound here tends to extend most viciously into all fields of sexuality.

Everything that we endeavor to experience on this level of form, here in the earthly world, bears that stamp not readily seen by the average man. Ego meant it to be this way. For it does bear an uncanny resemblance of our perceived "Fall from Grace," or, if you wish, our "loss" of Heaven.

Even the loving caresses we share in the coming together of two people during the sexual act all harken back to both souls trying to become one in some kind of earthbound oneness. Sexual coitus itself is indeed the ego's bland, fleeting, and inconsequential vision of what our minds should feel like in Heaven. Albeit on this level, the sensation remains a pale shadow, a futile and limited imitation of what the real thing is. Transcendence it is most certainly not. And if this need for coupling is not completed out of any idea of real love, there will remain with one, however temporarily, a sad and on occasion bitter aftertaste of something missing that cannot seem to be readily pinpointed and remedied. Even the whole notion that we have the need of separation extends to the birth of our offspring. They become the ones who must cast off their very own mother's unfailing love and protection at birth to become an "individual" physical entity. And honestly, can we declare that there exists any peace of mind or a lack of any conflict in the scenarios played out here? There is absolutely not, for peace of mind, tolerance, and understanding are what ego is NOT about.

The whole idea of duality is also characterized in the male and female roles that we engage ourselves in, for each successive lifetime that we imagine to live. Do you remember the very apt title we have frequently used between one another in our ongoing turmoil called the "battle of the sexes"? The roles played, in the long run, can diminish us significantly and make us willing pawns to ego's never-ending board game. Attempts such as how these games are played will seem to relegate our confused mind to exist in an extremely petulant, erratic, and mindlessly competitive state. And with that kind of mind-set, our lives become full of innuendo and fraught daily with tensions, sexual and otherwise.

Eventually, just when we begin to understand these face-offs a little more, we then come across some other anomalies created simply to enforce our separateness and apartness. The whole idea is aggravating for it tends to keep these "separate" souls at loggerheads by trying to find fault where there isn't any.

Let us take homosexuality, for instance, for this a classic case of one portion of humanity projecting fear and hatred on a small and select group. Homosexuality is considered a base anomaly, a perversion, a legitimate reason to find fault in a brother or sister. Homosexuality has existed since the dawn of man and does prevail in the animal kingdom to some degree. Even if it existed here on earth only to teach us that tiny little smidgen of tolerance, wouldn't it be a good enough reason for it to exist, and for us to learn from it?

During Yeshua's lifetime in Israel, one of the worst things a woman could ever do was to fornicate outside marriage. A sense of "righteous justification" or what was once called "righteous anger" would affect the populace, and death would be delivered speedily and without any mercy to the perpetrator in question. Of course we have to understand that this was the very worst thing that one could have done in first century Jewish society, with the sole exception of blasphemy. It generated in all people, not surprisingly, such negativity then as a case of child abuse or molestation would to-day. The resultant effects would still prove to be of a similar nature.

What lies in store, in the sordid child-molestation cases of to-day, for the perpetrator is a sure promise of long-term incarceration, exclusion, jail rape, revenge, and, very possibly, chemical castration. Also the death penalty is an option available in a number of places, and are all eschewed as a normal, acceptable, and justifiable judgment.

Perhaps we should be a little careful here and try to understand such brothers as being extremely sick and insane to a degree, if there is such a thing as degrees of insanity. But there are indeed those of us who would not consider even for a second becoming judge, jury, and righteous executioner at the drop of a hat when it is for offences against children. And if this is going to be the case, something there must be not quite right and so should be explored and questioned.

It is our deep, loving, understanding, and nurturing relationship with children that makes us very vulnerable, for it is indeed a special relationship. This must come as a surprise or shock to us, for even such a protective veneer can, and will, on a fairly regular basis be seen to degrade into obsession. Moreover, what is obsession itself but a subtle extension of fear now so readily seen in the public's pedophilic mania of today?

Children are a reminder for us, a symbol of our true nature as pure spirit, portraying within themselves all that beautiful single-minded innocence of our hidden Final Emergence. They are then seen only in the light of being perpetually forgiven, a true blessing from above, sacred and beyond sanction and akin to the gods, for they are in their own particular way inviolate. But were each and every one of us all not children at one time? So, careful we must be here, for this is an old territory where ego reigns and triumphs on a very regular basis. It, my friends, is one of those battlefields where fear, guilt, anger, attack, judgment, and murder are competing to be lords of the moment.

The Buddha, one time during one of his enduring lessons, asked his own disciples a very simple question regarding children. He asked them whether it was right to show more compassion for a dead child on the street than for a dead adult in similar circumstances. The answer was no! He chose this situation because he knew that his disciples would opt for this wrong answer, which would, naturally, be based on their senses and not the Buddha's bigger picture.

The world of the child molester and his victims is a horrific one. It is a world of aberration where guilt reigns and fear descends to newer levels, where any action can be justified and accounted for. But all actions in this lost nether region are actions where no light can penetrate, not until the light within can be recognized and shared. To the prospective child molester within our midst, and there must be quite a few, I have only these hopefully inspired words to share:

"You were created out of Love and Light a long time ago and in your darkening horizon, a fear of loss began to grow and dwell in your heart. You could not recognize yourself at first, and will not do so until you regain your connection with your Guide. For the loss incurred was the source of your primal guilt. You see in a child, one loved by all, the source of your fear. Yes, your fear is the loss of Innocence and you have now forgotten how to reconnect with it. But Innocence is of the healing Mind and by your actions; you have distanced yourself from your own healing. You try in vain to take back by force, that innocence you insist on having but you fail, for innocence is not of the physical or material level. Thus by your actions, you have created more guilt and by doing so, have delayed your own return."

If every man alive could consider and understand the results of their actions in play, then I believe this benighted place would cease to exist. It would have no reason to exist and we then could all go home. Knowing the results of our own actions beforehand is knowledge, and knowledge coexisting with experience gives us our wisdom.

However, wisdom alone will not lead us home, for it needs one more ingredient that acts as our catalyst and it pertains to the nature of the Holy Spirit. In wisdom and love we find that the key is Truth. It is this Truth that will set every single man free to return home finally.

We must remind ourselves that sex is not the "real McCoy." It was never meant to be, but it serves as a pale imitation in the memory, a timeless fleeting shadow of recognition, of what our true unadulterated Coalescence with God must be like.

Raymond Pratt
Samhain 2006

Chapter 21
The Veils of Forgetfulness

*E*arlier we touched upon the secret veils and subtle smoke-screens that were created intentionally to hide us from our Parent. The Veils can only be representative of every single wrong decision that was made by us with ego's input shortly after we "relinquished" our eternal home and all that it stood for. The veils, however, were created by us and with ego's misrepresentation also, so that he could pretend to successfully hide us from an "angry" God intent on His "Righteous Retribution." The veils covering our faulty decisions would then ensure that each and every one of those defective decisions we had opted for would be conveniently forgotten. This would happen at the very same moment as another veil came tumbling down, while the next incorrect choice had been acted out. This was to be a sensational master stroke for ego! It had almost managed, by this time, to wipe our minds totally clean of our uniquely spiritual nature, but not quite completely.

Because this could only be a totally new situation for a wayward soul, all subsequent decisions made by it would be based on this newly acquired state of mind, namely fear. It was indeed partly because of this same new state of mind that all decisions made by this "lost" soul would have to be questionable and highly suspect. And this can only be the case because of the nature of ego's now not-so-secret agenda.

We must remember that all this could never have happened without our own specific consent, willing or otherwise. But no matter what happened, there would be a significant and insistent blocking of the Great Rays of God, instigated by ego's vituperative whisperings and our built-in, made-to-measure "fear apparatus."

This, in effect, has served ego's purpose extremely well for tens of thousands of years and many hundreds of fruitless life-times. For all that, we became, in general, unaware of this not so apparent blockage, and so, totally misguided, we would continue on our merry way, round and around, spinning our wheels but going absolutely nowhere fast.

We did say that the Great Rays were blocked, but that is only partially true. It is not in the Nature of Our Father to leave us stranded and alone, so He extended Himself out to us through the Holy Spirit. It is this most significant Ray itself that we can avail of the Voice or Remembrance of God and is our ever-present Guide. So it is this Guide, the Holy Spirit, that does indeed manage to penetrate all the veils and nebulous creations that were surreptitiously conceived in error. This Voice can be called upon at any time, but we must acknowledge it willingly and wholeheartedly. The Great Ray light that comes from the Holy Spirit is pure unadulterated Truth (as opposed to perception) or if you wish, the Voice or Word of God. This Knowledge would be the first of a number of effective divine instruments that we would use to nullify the continuous and stultifying effects of the last created and closest veils to us.

The veils that I will consider here are but a few of many that do exist. Some are interchangeable; some are delicately interwoven and even rely on other veils such as guilt and fear. But after the first three or four veils, the order of precedence is not so necessary to follow. For after the removal of the Veil of Guilt, the Holy Spirit's guidance will be so prevalent in your mind that it will be quite difficult to choose a less direct path home. As we become aligned with the Oneness, the veils disappear. It is only when we diverge and continue to see ourselves as distinctly separate and apart that the veils reappear, as they are a creation of our own selves and ego.

What is important to us is that anytime one of the veils is raised, more and more of the Great Rays are available to us.

These Great Rays are mentioned in *A Course in Miracles*, in chapter 11, the introduction to "God or the Ego" on page 193.

The Veil of Ignorance

Ignorance is most definitely the very first veil that will have to be removed from us, because without its removal, there can be no appreciation for the existence outside the temporal world for a higher-minded spiritual world. It leaves us by choice Godless and totally subject to the mighty minions of what the Gnostic, and dualistic-minded French Cathars of old called Rex Mundi, or King of the World. That, my good friends, can only mean to me another name for our old friend, ego. Materialism is ignorance, self-interest is ignorance, complacency is ignorance, and our fear of the Lord is ignorance that is also sustained and complemented by the actions of another veil. Atheism, the ongoing refusal to believe in a God, is sheer unadulterated ignorance. It is, evidently, represented to us on the Jewish Kabalistic "Tree of Evil" (as opposed to the "Tree of Life") as one of the lowest and base spheres of existence.

When we overcome ignorance, we are just that little bit closer to the complete Godhead with Its healing and peace-inducing Rays. This is a relatively easy veil to lift by simply appreciating the existence of our Creator as a Loving Parent and striving to replace Him in His proper place in every aspect of our lives. It is only then that we find ourselves in new territory; this new territory is what we will call AWARENESS.

The Veil of Fear

Fear is the monster that all of us are subject to at any given time. Fear is so debilitating that it causes us to project outwards, toward our neighbor in the event of a perceived need to "attack." It can possibly be used to create an adversary or an enemy, for instance. It can also be used to project inward onto ourselves and to viciously attack our own esteem and self-worth.

Fear of God is an accompanying and attached veil that is so complete, and so interconnected with guilt and ignorance, that it has the tremendous capability of blocking out many of the Great Rays. So many people will be tempted to end their sojourns here at this point, but a simple lack of perseverance is not and cannot be a bona fide reason to halt our advancement. It is with this veil itself that most of us will have the most severe and demanding problems trying to erase it. But beyond it lies something potent and very necessary but totally lacking in this world. Consequently, this lack is proof positive of a world in turmoil, a world with so little love present in it.

"A world without fear is a world full of love."

The key to this insidious veil will be found in the far-reaching and absolutely genuine forgiveness as taught in *A Course in Miracles*. It neutralizes the idea of fear very quickly and prepares us for the next step to be released, which has been always been fear's closest ally.

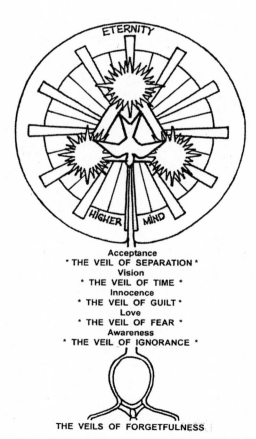

Acceptance
* THE VEIL OF SEPARATION *
Vision
* THE VEIL OF TIME *
Innocence
* THE VEIL OF GUILT *
Love
* THE VEIL OF FEAR *
Awareness
* THE VEIL OF IGNORANCE *

THE VEILS OF FORGETFULNESS

As we continue to remove these blocks from our journey home, the Holy Spirit may give us new tools that suit our "individual" abilities, and some may even be quite novel. In my case, it seems that I was given a kind of vision, but spelled with a small "v." This jewel of a gift seems to activate occasionally when I am talking with a person whose fears about something personal are not conducive to having the fear released. It would seem that another part of my mind instantly sees the result without prompting, like a bolt out of the sky. It is so shockingly complete and certain that it does seem to make my head spin and there seems to be no time lapse perceived between the fear declared and the result seen. The whole experience is so new to me that I am still trying to get used to it.

LOVE is the territory now available to all spiritual wayfarers who have managed to effectively raise this heartbreak of a veil.

The Veil of Guilt

It was this veil of Guilt that was the prime cause of the previous veil of Fear, for it is always going to be the natural progression that continually follows guilt. Just as the opposite of fear can only be love, guilt has an opposite that comes into play after the removal of this veil. We are living, believe it or not, in a continuous dream world! If I happen to commit a crime against you in my dream, can it reasonably be said that I must have committed it? And now, should I be punished for this same perceived transgression also? We all spring from the same "quelle," the same eternal Source in which we all exist as integral and interrelated parts of each other. So if my tooth hurts me occasionally, do I happen to take a small mallet to the offending tooth? Do I proceed then to knock it and a couple of other remaining good teeth out, subsequently causing me to suffer that much more unnecessary distress and pain? Hardly!

Much of the guilt that we encounter is so embedded within us that we are inclined to believe that it is part and parcel of our nature. This is not true at all, for this guilt comes from the wrong decisions that we made a long time ago with ego's machinations. We feel guilty because we left our Loving Parent without as much as a by your leave, so how could we feel any other way?

This is what the Course in Miracles says about guilt:

"The ego is not a traitor to God, to Whom treachery is impossible. But it is a traitor to you who believe that you have been treacherous to your Father. That is why the undoing of guilt is an essential part of the Holy Spirit's teaching. For as long as you feel guilty you are listening to the voice of ego…"

We are altogether too inclined to be very hard on ourselves, and if we are to use this as a measuring stick, it can only be assumed that we will in no way embrace forgiveness for our brothers' idiosyncrasies. So we have to forgive our brothers and by this we are released and forgiven. No more guilt then needs to be encountered regarding God, our brothers, and ourselves as we learn to finally raise this burdensome curtain. Now, it is a wonderful expanse that can be viewed extending to a scintillating horizon. Now we can relate positively to the substantial amount of the Godhead's Great Rays that are shining through. The light, it feels, is blended with so much more Compassion and Love that it seems to manifest before our eyes in a completely new terrain, a territory so far-fetched and alien in the past to us. It has been many eons since we felt that we were denizens of this place, the wayfarers' Shangri La. Welcome back, for this is the land of the pristine snows.

This is the land of INNOCENCE

There will no doubt be other veils to be removed, some not too hard and some relatively easy, ranging, for instance, from consciousness, duality, etc., prior to reaching the final veil. But at this stage of the journey, the correct decisions we make will be prompted by the Holy Spirit and NOT by ego, which previously had made the promptings when we were traveling the other way, from magnitude to littleness. For it is now that this whole insane notion of separateness and being apart is ultimately being made redundant.

We are approaching a point where the idea of returning home without our brother is not an option to be considered even for a moment. Now it is only the forgotten Voice of God that can be heard, clear, distinct, and reverberating in our fast-cleansing mind. For now our choices will be so blatantly obvious, as we rapidly approach our Reality. We will then finally drop all our pretences of what we thought we were, to embrace the next veil.

The Veil of Time

Acknowledging that time is a manmade variable, which uses the past to trap us in an unnecessary future, is a major step in corrected thinking. Yes, time is a veil that is used against us in many ways. Its chief purpose is to make us believe that we are unimportant and have only a small amount of time allotted to us in one singular life. Time even distorts how we see our brother, for with it, we can find no end to the reasons where we can blame and project. This is possible because the past will conjure a variety of reasons why our brother is "guilty" and needs to be "corrected."

Perhaps if our brother is perceived by us as having a "guilty" past, there then has to be some form of "punishment," one that needs to be served on what we now see as the perceived guilty party. The notion of punishment means that we are now inflicting a future on our brother, but in actual fact this is not the case; we are indeed inflicting a future on ourselves. That, readers, is what is stopping our return home to the Father.

"When we see the past in our brother instead of the eternal present, we inflict a future on ourselves that we don't need!"

Time is also used to make us believe that we have a long way home to travel, when in reality, our Home lies right behind that very veil we speak of. Ego's ploys are seemingly endless and we always have to be on our guard against such machinations. This Veil of Time is also connected and woven intricately into the strands of the Veil of Separation. These two extraordinary veils are very closely allied to each other, for when we indulge in the notion of time, we see something that needs to be healed. And when we see separation, we are precluding the existence of one great single soul indigenous to all mankind.

Time is NOT of the essence, and eternity is and has always existed in the now. When Yeshua said:

"The Kingdom of God is at hand,"

He meant that the Kingdom was always available in the present and at the present moment. There is no subtle interface between time and eternity because one is real and the other is not, so our correct choice leads us to the next veil that lies in waiting for us.

The Veil of Separation

Here we are knowledgeable, fearless, guilt-free, and innocent. We are very able and capable of continuing our journey home, and the Veil of Separation is a particularly important veil to raise because it brings us in touch with Yeshua, our divine Brother. This leaves us in the eternal regions of the SONSHIP, to put it simply. In other words, it tries to convey to us that we are, with Yeshua, part and parcel of the original Holy Trinity. This is where God the Father and God the Son have always wanted us to be. Just like our own Brother Yeshua, who was God's Son incarnate, we are also the Father's sons and daughters in training. To be brutally honest altogether, it would seem that we have located ourselves in some form of self-inflicted reeducation camp for perpetuity.

But at this wholesome, august, and rarified level, we are so loved and loving; we radiate the completeness of all of the emanations inherent in the Prince of Peace. We are now ready to join with Them in the Trinity and to take our rightful place in the Sonship.

This birthright is ready and available; it always has been, to all of humankind, through Yeshua's insightful Resurrection. This regal birthright of ours, so divinely unique and astounding that it is, could only be fulfilled by our being a blessed part of the Second Person of the Holy Trinity.

Raymond Pratt
Mean Fomhair 2006

Chapter 22
What is the Soul?

*W*hen my mother, Marie, was very young, in actual fact when she was a child, she told her mother one time that she would marry an American. I can see now, very clearly in my mind's eye, my grandmother's incredulous look and quick retort to such a remark,

"An American? Go away ou' that now an' don't you be blaggardin' me with your carry on!"

And marry an American my mother would go on to do, but hardly now out of any sense of spite.

Souls are peculiar things, and people in all honesty, especially those of the Christian persuasions, have this inclination to think of their individual selves numbering in the billions. The general consensus nowadays is that we all have soul mates and to a certain point, we indeed can consider this to be somewhat partially true. But then if opposites do attract, however, and similar souls repel, we must indeed then get ready for one huge battle royal. For if we are to succumb to the wiles and wishes of our opposite, or cannot work with our like-minded brethren, what are we then supposed to work with, for what do we think we have left in common?

There is a commonality in souls that reaches deep down into the dense and entwining grassroots that lie at the foundation of our existence. But first I would like to explore the popular and favored notion that opposite souls attract.

The idea that opposites attract is like the idea of the yin and yang, the positive and the negative, and the male and female. They are, in every case, descriptions of two of something becoming one, a this and a that joining to become the other. This idea then will have to be seen for what it is, classified in its correct context. They tend to be symbols of division and duality and in being so are of no importance or of any consequence to us. For the simple fact that opposites do attract shows us that ego, our demented mentor, has this persistent and repetitive need to keep on creating discord in all our relationships with each other. Who else would consider for a moment that by bringing opposites together, it would cease the eternal fluctuations and bring about real peace?

By doing this so well, ego succeeds in keeping us firmly rooted to the timeline that we are by now so very well acquainted with, some nondescript place where we honestly don't want or need to be. Brothers, real peace can only derive from a mind at peace with itself; it is not indigenous to this level of form. This is and remains but a world of duality, a world of countless variations vying for your credence and each and every one born out of a faulty thought process in crisis. Now let me give you a little fact!

"There is only one soul and we all share it whether we like or not."

True, we can see ourselves as a bunch of separate entities milling around and bumping into each other and that is how ego has managed to manipulate us for eons. The old idea of seeing ourselves with separate identities is only partly true and in so far as the idea that those individual holograms of the same creation are separate. But the simple reality is that they are NOT, and why is this? All souls are one and the same; they exist as exact replicas of the original soul, which itself was created by Our Father on a different level, before the beginning of time.

Interesting? Well, how about if I suggested to you that the original soul is still in Heaven, safe and sound, fast asleep, and constantly dreaming of exile? Should that not give us a little peace of mind somehow? The Holy Spirit is always right there beside us, whispering quietly and oh! so gently in our ear to wake us up. He would never, ever consider trying to shake us awake and no one should.

Let us compare ourselves to sunbeams for a little moment and see Our Father as the Sun. We try to build fences around our own sunbeam to try and keep out the other sunbeams. But it is a ludicrous effort and one that has no effect on anyone else, and it only keeps our true nature stymied. You cannot corral what is of the Father, but there is absolutely nothing stopping us from trying, at least until we start to wake up.

It is our own recognition, with the Holy Spirit's help, by waking up to the full realization of what we genuinely are that counts in any event. Then all should gradually unfold and as the joyfully enthralling metamorphosis it should be, not some massive, traumatic, and numbingly overpowering event.

That is the very same reason why God, our Father in Heaven, speaks to us through Yeshua, His Son and the Holy Spirit, His Voice or Holy Remembrance. As for everything else, it must be done in stages through the element of forgiveness or otherwise.

The soul is totally indestructible for it is of God's making and there is NOTHING that can prevail against it. Not even our petty attempts to cast it aside from lifetime to lifetime affect it. It simply HAS to find its way Home one way or another, because it was conceived perfectly in eternity. Thus its creation is its own Homing Device and yes, we are all indeed coming along for the ride, each and every one of us whether we like it or not and sooner or later.

To recognize the soul correctly for how it relates to us is to recognize a Truth, a Truth that can have a lasting effect on our ultimate spiritual realization. It gives us the opportunity to see beyond the walls we have created to keep us apart from our brother.

With regard to the notion that opposites attract and that we have soul mates, we need to add another subtle ingredient. The attraction of opposites is the "attraction of infliction" where those past perceived slights needed to be acted on. Remember we mentioned:

"Do not let the past inflict a future on you that you do not need."

Any forgiveness of old remembered slights and old perceived abuses by soul mates or otherwise are, under these circumstances, a tremendous leap ahead, for there within it truly lies a holy relationship.

So for this reason it is immensely important to see our relationships in a totally different light. Where one tends to be the abused victim in an issue, it just might also be the scripted chance for this soul to advance, if correctly understood through the Higher Mind. And so where that perceived offending soul may be considered to be the agent provocateur, that very same soul may be also creating a holy relationship for its victim. Then it all stands to reason that what we perceive on this level of form is not all cut and dried. This shows that there is a real need for all souls to interact thoroughly within their own appointed "separateness" and "apartness." For it is there that lie the keys to their kingdom, their Reality, and their original Oneness. So where opposites do seem to attract, it really is about old lessons coming back again and again to haunt us, for they are repeat lessons that need to be recognized and accomplished.

A holy relationship can be likened to a progression to a higher grade because all of the old slights that have been effectively forgiven. Or possibly it might be akin to receiving a more comprehensive degree for the sole and express purpose of continuing. But it is one that is open indiscriminately to all souls, available at any given time, and one that we must always need to strive toward and attain.

A holy relationship is not and cannot be compared to the "Holy Instant," for it does tend to involve for us the release of our brothers using scripted time and because of that, there is a release for us from more repetition. Where the Holy Instant appears and differs from it is that time is immaterial, for it always operates outside of time and is solely of the Holy Spirit. This is how we must now see our brother, for it is all about Recognizance.

Recognizance will then bring us into the realms of the Higher Mind where the Holy Spirit helps us to quietly remember completely our part in the Completeness. It is there that we unlock our innocence, for the eternal soul cannot be anything but innocent in the eyes of God. And what is innocent and guilt-free in the eyes of God must be accepted as the only Final Truth for the "separated" soul.

When this is accepted, we have then no reason or need to be

here anymore, for this is the Gate of Heaven. This is our Resurrection of the Mind, and this is where be become rejoined with the Loving Presence.

Raymond Pratt
Samhain 2006

Chapter 23
The Secret, in Response to a Good Friend

*T*oday I came across a catchy movie on DVD called *The Secret*, Its role is to show the secret to happiness, health, wealth, and love for all. Supposedly, its contents have been hidden from us for hundreds of years by the hands of some kind of obscure illuminati who held onto it very closely. *The Secret* promises the world and more to us, and for this reason alone I decided to watch it for content. As the movie was given to me by a very good friend, I did endeavor to watch all of it, so this is my letter to my good friend, Mark:

Dear Mark,

I would like to take this opportunity to thank you for sharing with me what you might seem to consider as the fountain of the secret to your success. Yes, I have indeed heard much about this new movie, *The Secret*, from others and I was very thankful that you made it available to me. I found the movie a little longwinded and fairly intriguing, albeit the shock tactic format it was delivered in seems to promise more than it had to offer.

We have been good friends for a long time now, and it does seem that paths do reach points of divergence. But this is quite a natural process in motion as we seek to continue the quest for what we scripted in this life. I can truly understand that you do sincerely wish to see me comfortably well-off, happy, and successful, and I do appreciate that. The movie, I will have to admit, had me making my own list of priorities to focus on and I still have it plainly written on a big white board as was suggested. I also found a lesson to be learnt from this board and shamefacedly decided that I would show it to you and the world.

Below is my wish list that I have considered most carefully in order of precedence, starting from the least important to the most important. I have also notated each wish with what part of the mind I was using, higher or lower, when I decided:

I want a Jaguar XK8 coupe	Ego
I want a house like Xxx Xxxxx's	Ego
I want to earn $500,000 per year	Ego
I want to be a successful author	Ego
I am happy, healthy, and thin	Ego
As long as I give, I will never want	Split mind
I want to touch people's lives with Inner Peace and outer joy	Holy Spirit
I want to be always grateful	Holy Spirit
I want to forgive and love the world	Holy Spirit
I want, in this life, to go Home to my Father	Holy Spirit.

Yes, I did say *shamefacedly*, because when I began to focus on what I wanted, I perceived a small little cloud in my mind. It was as though all the work that I had done for my own spiritual self-improvement through the help of the Holy Spirit had evaporated into thin air, and had caused me to spiritually gag. Something vague was still niggling me and it would cast my mind back to Yeshua's Parable involving "eyes of needles" and such. But I didn't give too much notice to it, at least not until the following morning.

Early today, I started to do my morning lesson from my well-thumbed workbook *A Course in Miracles*. It was lesson # 50 and titled "I am sustained by the Love of God," and, Mark, it all then became so crystal clear to me. I have taken an excerpt from the lesson to reinforce how I feel about the whole subject.

LESSON 50

"Here is the answer to every problem that will confront you, today, tomorrow, and throughout time. In this world, you believe you are sustained by everything but God. Your fate is placed in the most trivial and insane symbols; pills, money, "protective" clothing, influence, prestige, being liked, knowing the "right people," and an endless list of forms of nothingness that you endow with magical powers.

All these things are replacements for the Love of God. All these things are cherished to ensure a body identification. They are songs of praise to the ego. Do not put your faith in the worthless. It will not sustain you.

Only the Love of God will protect you in all circumstances. It will lift you out of every trial, and raise you high above all the perceived dangers of this world into a climate of perfect peace and safety. It will transport you into a state of mind that nothing can threaten, nothing can disturb, and where nothing can intrude upon the eternal calm of the Son of God.

Put not your faith in illusions. They will fail you. Put all your faith in the Love of God within you; eternal, changeless, and forever unfailing. This is the answer to whatever confronts you..."

Today, Mark, this being the 8th of December 2006, this is my solemn declaration of release from the belief in idols. This is my acknowledgement of the truth about myself.

Mark, I thank you for your honest concern for me and I know that it's from the heart. However, there is a time when every man will have to travel a lonely road, but only until he meets and recognizes his Guide.

This morning, I met and recognized my Guide and He endeavored to show me "the secret" pitfalls that lay before me. He again called on me for my unwavering vigilance and I came to the decision that He was right and that I was, perhaps, a little off course again for the umpteenth time. But thanks again, Mark.

Your Friend, Ray.

The problem altogether with those choices that I had made became very easy to understand, and just by knowing ego's ways, about ninety percent would probably have been fulfilled. Well, at least the first unimportant ones would have been. But you can see here clearly, that by my choices, my mind was split simply by trying to serve myself (and ego) and the Holy Spirit and thus confusion would reign. Vigilance is always needed in situations like these, for a split mind can serve no master. This then has to be a classic case of a split mind, so the results would end up for all as meaningless.

Don't misunderstand me. I am not decrying money, power, and fame and all the good things of life. They are only idols and it is just that I wonder if they play into the hands of the Holy Spirit, or our old buddy, ego, again.

Raymond Pratt
Nollaig 2006

Chapter 24
Was Yeshua Married?

*W*ith all the speculation running rife over the past year about the contents of a recent publication, namely The Da Vinci Code, some clarification might be sorely needed. We have to be most careful on what should be designated as fact, possibility, probability or fiction and what are the elements we tend to use that convey those possibilities and probabilities. Adding to all this, what instances exist that portray to us a common resonance?

There is probably no doubt at all that Yeshua knew of Mary Magdalene, as the little village of Magdala (Hebr. Migdal, a tower) lay just a short distance inland from the Sea of Galilee and is still located about halfway between Caparnaum (Kfar Nahoom) in the Gennesaret area and the Graeco-Roman city of Tiberias. This city of Tiberias was then shunned by all religious Jews due to its being built on the remains of an ancient Jewish graveyard. It was strictly forbidden for rabbis or any sect members of the priestly persuasion, Pharisee, Sadducee, or Levite to walk over interred bodies as it made them unclean. It is For this reason it would take perhaps a century or more to pass before this ban could ever be lifted.

Herod Antipas, after living his young life under the "patronage" (he was, during his youth, in reality, a royal hostage) of the Roman Caesars, Augustus and Tiberius respectively, built the city of Tiberias and named it in honor of the reigning Caesar.

Tiberias is not a town mentioned in the Gospels as a distinct place where Yeshua had visited. Neither was the other rather large Graeco-Roman town of Sepphoris in upper Galilee and for a good reason, as a significant proportion of the population in both towns were of the Gentile persuasion. Sepphoris did lie no more than five miles northwest from Nazareth and was where Mary, the mother of

Yeshua, had been born. During Yeshua's early teenage years, approximately in 10 C.E., Sepphoris went through a major reconstruction that would have been a decent source of income for some of the surrounding villages. An income as such would probably have been earned then, by providing all the necessary skilled and semi-skilled labor, the carpenters and stone-masons needed, all with growing families to feed.

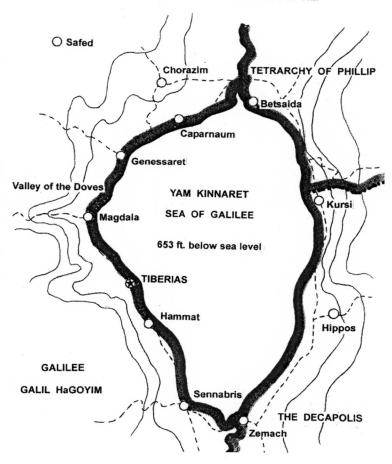

THE SEA OF GALILEE AREA about 30 C.E.

The city of Tiberias, on the other hand, was a day's walk away on the lake and the northern capital of Herod the Great's son,

Herod Antipas. After the sad demise of John the Baptist, Yeshua would have had some need to keep a relatively close eye on him, whom He called "that fox." Herod was a rather weak ruler and prone to being quite superstitious. He was also known to have thought that Yeshua might very well have been the reincarnation of the dead John, whom he had earlier executed as a face-saving device. The pertinent knowledge available to him was that John's followers were now in the process of seeking the new local teacher. This would exacerbate Herod's worries for he knew of Yeshua's unique work no more than ten miles away in the town of Caparnaum.

Magdala lay at the very bottom of the Valley of the Doves, a very pretty outcrop that descends down from the Galilean uplands, toward the beautiful lakeside that is actually 653 feet below sea level. The village lay close to the lakeshore and was noted for its very mild winters. An easterly wind called the Sharkiyah was also known to blow down quite suddenly from the Golan Heights and across the lake during the short winters. Such an occasion happening is told in the Gospel when Yeshua walked on the water to His Apostles who were in dire fear of drowning.

Yeshua would have passed close by to Magdala on his journeys west to Nazareth and Cana (Kfar Kana) in the hill country. It is most likely that He would not have had a reason to spend too much time in the village of Magdala, (there are a number of times mentioned in the Gospels, as in Matt. 14:34, Mark 6:53 and Mark 8:10 for the general area and in Matt. 15:39 for the town itself) unless it was to see Mary of Magdala, whom we do know He was very fond of. However, the village did lie quite close to the "fox's den" of Herod's in Tiberias, no more than four and a half miles away. For this reason alone, it must have tended to make Yeshua's visits here to be rather on the short side. Herod, with all his continuing interest in Yeshua's miracle work, His abilities, and possible claim to the hotly contested and vacant title of Messiah, could provide a serious threat to His Ministry if Herod thought the need might arise (Luke 13:31-35).

Yeshua would choose Capernaum because it was a border town of approximately 1,500 souls within a few miles of the frontier on the northern Jordan River. It was a town that drew its income from fishing on the lake as well as agricultural produce. It was also different in that it was a border crossing, and in this way would enable Yeshua access to the many Gentiles of the neighboring countries. This is one of the reasons that we find in the Bible many of Yeshua's healing works acknowledged by the non-Jews of the area. In fact the full name used for Galilee in Hebrew is "Ha Galil HaGoyim," The District of the Foreigners. This may stem from the fact that many of those Jews returning from their captivity in Babylon probably had no choice but to settle here. And this was probably due to much resistance encountered from the Judeans further south who now found them, after three generations away in a foreign empire, a little different.

The few Jews who had managed to evade captivity in Judea would now be a more substantial number, and would have seen themselves as the real torchbearers of Abraham's seed, belief system, and lineage.

Tax collection was another distinct peculiarity of Capernaum. Remember the tax collectors in the Bible? They were the ancient customs and excise agents of the day and had free reign over what they could overcharge for taxes. It was for only as long as their fickle Roman overlords received their goodly portion. However, this led obviously to corruption on a fairly large scale by the hated tax-collectors and some occasional rioting, hence their ostracism by most of the local populace. The more fortunate side to this frontier location was that, should the need arise for Yeshua to take leave in a hurry, an escape route was readily available across the Jordan River, which was fordable north of Bethsaida. For here lay the Tetrarchy of Phillip on the east side of the river, and although he was a close relation of Herod Antipas, he was considered a more tolerant ruler.

Yeshua was to be found in the Temple in Jerusalem discussing various tenets of Judaic Law at the tender age of approximately twelve or so. While He may have been celebrating some kind of Bar Mitzvah, He knew He had a special duty to complete. But His Own statement made regarding the nature of the God of His father's as being His Own Father in Heaven, even at such an age, would have been seriously considered to be anathema and blasphemous. And it is this question He asked that raises questions, provided that this question is indeed true:

> "Why have you looked for Me, do you not know I should be about My Father's business?" (Luke 2:49).

This was His remark to His anxious parents when He went missing for three days. Oddly, Mary's question was:

> "Son, why have You dealt with us? Behold, Your father and I have looked for you in sorrow." And He said to them, "Why have you looked for Me, did you not know that I must be about My Father's Business?" (Luke 2:48-49).

Mary mentions Yeshua's earthly father, but Yeshua mentions His Heavenly Father and this may have been a play on words to stymie any blasphemous intention that might be taken up by any of the surrounding onlookers and wise men.

Yeshua's overpowering duty, it would seem, could and would override any emotional attachments to his parents even at this early age. It also would prove to be just as agonizing during His ministry when the family would be dismissed out of hand by His remark that was almost a rebuke:

> "Who is My mother, who are My sisters and brothers?" (Matt. 12:46-50).

It is on one occasion that His relations wanted to take Him out of the spotlight by possibly claiming Him as not quite right mentally. It could have been a ploy to save His life from a stoning for blasphemy, by excusing His actions with the statement:

> "He is beside Himself."

There was also the possibility that the extended family of Yeshua, who were now being left aside for His newly created Apostleship, had their own, not so secret political/religious aspirations in mind. But such familial considerations could prove to be acrimonious within the extended family members of His original home in Nazareth, probably initiating His desire to be free to do His necessary work. His Nazarene neighbors could also pose some problems as He did mention that the Lord's prophets would never be recognized in their home towns.

Yeshua was aware that the emotional ties people engage in could be anathema or conducive to what His mission was and what was necessary to be done. Could it be that this enigmatic mystic, this itinerant teacher, this vagabond rabbi, chose this life-style to counteract the temptation of any kind of close potential human relationship?

It is quite unlikely, for it was through those very same relationships that Yeshua saw His Father at work. He did not need to offer some potential mate stability or any vague notion of it, as He had come to change that very status quo. The only thing Yeshua honestly had to offer the populace was His supremely compassionate and charismatic presence and enunciations, and of course His miracle work, which was always based on faith and forgiveness.

Yeshua was, however, also quite aware that if any emotional bond happened to be sealed through, take for instance, marriage, it should be nurtured and cherished. He had some straightforward remarks to say, for those who had ears to listen, about marriage and divorce when asked by Peter. He rebuked males for their hard hearts, as men, He implied, had it easier where divorce was an issue. Tolerance, we know, for women at this time, was sadly lacking and still Yeshua managed to state clearly and unquestionably the correct approach to His disciples:

"What God has created, let no man pull asunder." (Matt. 19:3-12)

So what can we surmise from what we know?

1. Yeshua knew from an early age that He was special in that he had a unique mission to complete for His Father, regardless of the heartache to His parents, family, or friends of which He had many.

2. Between twelve and approximately thirty years of age, there is absolutely no mention of Yeshua. This could well have been the time of His Midrash, a time of deep and compelling studies of the Judaic Scriptures, written and oral, of which Yeshua, it seems, had a lasting and comprehensive knowledge. Midrash is still practiced by religious Jews to this day as a means of endorsing oneself to God's Plan.

It could also have been a time when He was married and raising a family. The early Church fathers were so adamant on many occasions about excising what could be classified or construed as "damning" evidence that we cannot be sure. That very same total lack of evidence could even imply or insinuate the possibility that Yeshua was indeed a married man.

Yeshua might also, during this formative time, have traveled the twenty miles or so from the capital city of Jerusalem to Qumran. Near the low northern end of the Dead Sea (Hebrew: Yam HaMelkh, the Sea of Salt) was a community that Yeshua could have spent time with, the Essene community. The Essenes, who thought the temple priests corrupt, lived a strict and chaste life. None of the initiates there were allowed to be married. However, this does not insinuate that Yeshua was not married. But it may contribute to the idea that because He was married, He would not have been allowed to become an Essene.

3. Although Jewish men were supposed to fulfill their obligation to God by being fruitful and multiplying, a thirty-three-year-old non-married male would have been a quite rare and unusual occurrence and would be a talking point. However, we mentioned that the Essenes were chaste and did not marry at all. Neither did, we can suppose, John the Baptist, but there is no reason not to believe that he was either.

St. Paul/Saul, the "Apostle" of the "conversion on the road

to Damascus" fame was another religious man who supposedly did not marry. Or maybe it is simply that an earlier wife may have passed away, prior to his historic conversion. The many letters ascribed to Paul have certainly been taken out of context. And a number of suggestions pertaining to his own sexual orientation have been unnecessarily called by some students into question, as if that should even matter. Nevertheless everything is, of course, subject to whether we are to believe whoever it was that penned the scripture. And there were many incidents where manuscripts were manipulated all on a fairly regular occasion, to suit the relevant needs of the prevailing times.

The women of Israel did respect their holy men as could be expected for the times at hand. But even in the days of the earlier prophets of the Old Testament (e.g. the prophets Hosea and Samuel) it was not out of the question to take a wife and have children. It was a very much expected way of fulfilling one's obligations to the Judaic Law.

If Yeshua had married, and He may very well have, He would have to have been totally committed to the relationship and He would never have considered at any stage, divorcing His prospective wife. Who knows, it may have been that one of His closest disciples was His wife. We know that He was particularly fond of the local woman who was on many occasions in His entourage and she was Mary Magdalene of Magdala.

When Mary Magdalene went to Yeshua's tomb after He was interred, she was very alone and found it empty. This is when she went to seek and tell Peter of the great news that the Lord was alive. And was she not the first one He appeared to? The simple notion that she was there at all at the grave points to a very prominent and significant fact easily overlooked. The fact is that only close members of a family were allowed, by Jewish Law, to enter the tomb. For anyone else, the entry would have made them unclean.

Even when Lazarus was brought back to life, it was not Ye-shua, His friend, who removed the entrance stone or entered the tomb for that matter, for Yeshua created the miracle from outside of the tomb. Thus, Lazarus was a friend but NOT a family member.

4. Although Yeshua was known to be, and would remain a compassionate and loving person in our lives, it is very important that He saw us all as brothers and sisters. He saw our intrinsic need to return Home to our Father and sexuality as part of the dualistic anomaly that only needed to be brought back to the Oneness. This can be seen clearly, on a number of occasions, in the one hundred and fourteen logions of the Gospel of St. Thomas of which a study is highly advised.

Yeshua saw sin as a temporary state of error, a case of missing the mark, so to speak. The one on one, close, personal, needy, and special ordinances needed to fulfill any kind of relationship in marriage might just have necessitated a need for a much more platonic relationship. Especially, if there might have been the case that the relationship was seen to come between His Father and His Ministry, which were one and the same. However, the whole notion of the existence of there being any offspring between Himself and some prospective wife is a moot point. As we have mentioned earlier, it would not have made His bloodline any holier, as holiness is only of the mind, not the body.

5. Yeshua's life was always in some kind of danger and He accepted this for Himself. Remember, He knew intimately of all that would happen to Him, for He had foretold it on a number of occasions to His Apostles, the Pharisees, and His disciples and followers. This is what He said to them:

"You can destroy this temple and in three days I will raise it up again!"

Truly this was not a situation where you would care to see the love of your life, the frail flower of your heart in any way, suffering such a traumatic agenda, even if it was perceived. But then again the supreme question may be how spiritually advanced was Mary Magdalene's mind under the regular tutelage of Yeshua? And was she made privy to such secrets like Thomas was, for Peter the Apostle does mention how much more He loved her over them?

Yeshua was and would always remain a caring and loving Being. He would always remain in our hearts as the Personification of Compassion. He could see the furthest extent of His Father's realm as the "Kingdom of Heaven within us." For He understood all must return in due course to their birthright, within the Source of all Oneness and Goodness.

Raymond Pratt
Bealtaine 2006

Chapter 25
The Magician and the Fool

*B*ack in the 1970s, I took a fairly respectable amount of interest in certain occult studies such as astrology, the Tarot, and pretty much anything that those peculiar fields had to offer. All had this innate tendency to intrigue me immensely. The Tarot deck really did fascinate me for its fine element of divination and the secret, obscure, and ancient knowledge that lay well hidden within its many symbols.

Basically the Tarot deck numbers seventy-four cards that are divided into two separate and very distinct decks. There are the Minor Arcana of fifty-two fairly regular cards and there is the smaller deck of twenty-two for the Major Arcana. The minor cards correspond to a normal pack of playing cards with kings, queens, jacks, and aces, but the major cards are particularly colorful, quite detailed and overflow profusely with arcane occult knowledge.

Generally speaking, one will find regular use of these cards in some sense productive, but only as in the nature of minds joined on this lower level of form. Perhaps then we must classify the Tarot cards express use by students as "magic" as opposed to "miracles," as has been taught in *A Course in Miracles*. However, what we can perceive in our lessons should be used constructively, in some way or another, whether it deigns to be for the further spiritual advancement of our brothers or for ourselves. In this case, I find that there is a lesson to be taught in the first two cards of the Major Arcana, those being of course card #0, "The Fool," and card #1, "The Magician."

The Fool is closely associated with decisions and paths to be considered and taken; he is the archetype of innocence and to the Magician's eyes, the personification of naïveté. The Magician sees

the Fool as life's pawn and may indeed be blinded by his own perceived ability. Is the Magician then involved in using his "creative" power? Or is there a chance he is abusing it. It depends how
we are going to interpret "creative," for can one really abuse that
which is creative? Nevertheless, these cards, where they are represented in a Tarot spread, pose and demonstrate as powerful symbols and significators at work, depending on their own particular
placement therein.

It is normal, too, that a great many like to compare themselves
to certain aspects inherent in the individual Tarot cards that they
can identify with. If we are left to personally choose which card to
pick, one can imagine that the choice must be plainly obvious. Or
can it be so obvious? Or is it that we are using perception again in
its confused light?

Yes, we are creators but it is not our function on this level to
create. Our function here is to submit and forgive, both necessary
entry perquisites prior to our returning to the Father. In the Real
World, our correct function is then to create within the conjoined
and expanded state of our Father's and Brother's Love. But not
here!

Now I would like you to take a very close look at the two cards
we are now discussing in any Rider-Waite tarot deck and see how
these two cards compare, and how or why they might differ. Then
try and see through whose eyes do we imagine that the cards are
now being seen. If we are focusing with the jaundiced eyes of ego,
then where does that put the Fool?

The Magician will need an audience, for it is only through
them that the minds are joined on some level of form, so there
must be some sense of manipulation. He also has the need of his
special identifying and ornate vestments simply to distinguish himself from his hushed and awed audience. He needs the necessary
tools of his trade just to create his "magic." He is trying to engage
and identify himself in a kind of "special relationship," with the
powers that be, through ceremony.

The Magician represented is continuously standing in one position facing the source of his power, that being his audience. This
symbolizes stasis, inertness, and the manifestation of worldly
power at a local level. The red roses so prevalent in this fanciful il-

lustration do suggest an element of passion for his trade. The special tools of his profession are the cup, the wand (or baton), and the pentacle (or coin) and sword because all of these tools symbolize the four basic elements of water, fire, earth, and air respectively. These tools are also astrological symbols and denote "opposition" and "square" aspects, (aspects of strife, adjustment, karma, and difficulty) when they are placed in certain positions. That for me tends to underline an attachment to the world.

The Fool, on the other hand, sees no reason to have an audience for he is closely in tune with his higher Mind. There is an inclination to carry very little, for then he can travel light. There is no call for special vestments and so, no sense of ostentation. He carries and displays in his left hand a white rose, suggesting the element of freedom, transformation, and possibly transcendence. He is shown to us stepping sprightly over a precipice and harboring on his face a distinct lack of the fear of the unknown. His look remains charismatic, a mind in total submission and strict abeyance to his own higher Mind. The Fool will take his leap of faith willingly, for he has withheld all decision and judgment, foregoing its obvious predictable result. He is now transcending from one level of form, for it is his forward movement that insinuates his advancement. The precipice can symbolize the Truth as well, and it stands alone, for it has to, as there is only one Truth that must always remain a constant. If Truth did not remain a constant, it would not really exist and so would not be a necessary element for humankind. Without Truth there would be no salvation for we would then be lost in our illusions.

The precipice also is the shift of consciousness for the Fool, so there is nothing of this world that can really hurt him. In the cloth sack that he carries over his right shoulder on a stick is his esoteric or hidden wisdom. Remember the stick or baton symbolizes fire, the same latent fire of the Paraclete, so the bag and carrying stick conjoined intimate his own connection and accessibility to the wisdom of the Holy Spirit.

The Magician commands the change to occur, and he alone decides what he needs as a result for proof. He sees his knowledge displayed without, and himself as the sole intermediary where none is needed, and so he is a kind of unnecessary middleman. His stance suggests that he is pure enough to act as a conduit or light-ning rod for the heavenly Power. But for him, only the results seem to always matter because his status, which can only be of a vari-able nature, is constantly decided by it. Thus he has a need of al-lies. But the Fool, he withholds decision. His acquired knowledge remains fully embraced, but hidden, for he is his own intermediary, and results do not and will not matter, for his own action is its re-sult.

The Magician is aware of the Fool and can only see him through worldly eyes for what he is NOT! As for the Fool, he re-mains totally unaware of the Magician for his individuality or apartness is being decentralized, while he finally coalesces on the Source of all Power that inhabits the higher Mind.

Readers, I do honestly think that if I should have that choice to make, I would then suffer to be the world's Fool rather than God's Impersonator!

Raymond Pratt
Samhain 2006

Epilogue

*N*ow it is with a sad heart that I begin to write these, our final chapters for the book. It has proved to be quite an interesting journey for all of us. I have led you on an exploration of well-documented fields and others in the exploratory stage, all in the sincere hope that it might prove a benefit to each and every one of you. Beliefs and their documentation are all very well for spiritual searchers on this road, but they all have to be well considered and effectively refined through the Divine Screening System of the Holy Spirit. The very necessary active ingredients and the main catalyst for this novel system will be availed of and effectively applied through our own higher mind usage; which happens, of course to involve Love and Forgiveness.

Our journey together not only involves ourselves alone but must include that distinctly sublime aspect of God, tangible to all at any given time.

I have mentioned perhaps once or twice before that I believe that this book was also scripted from a higher Source. I do believe that the higher Source saw a need for me to promulgate such an edition, past the weekly classes that I used to teach, all in the effort to reach a larger segment of the populace. If this is so, then there's a very good chance that now we have been given an opportunity to begin our journey home together, or are at least we can be considered to be en route. And if this is the case, we must be at that point in time where the Prodigal Son finally decides to return to His Father. This is about the halfway point that lies between the Alpha and the Omega points, whose return distance for the awakening soul keeps shrinking at a strikingly faster rate, all due to the corrections of the Holy Spirit.

We are at this moment now past the halfway mark with our new tools readily close at hand that will enable us finally to reach the Omega or return point and home. This we can quickly accomplish now and a great deal faster than from the time of "Our Fall" at the Alpha point, to the point in time where we make this most important decision of our lives.

Even if this was a decision made by us at this very instant, it is a significant step where time itself starts to become inconsequential. We should now happily rejoice for our final return to our Loving, Compassionate, and Waiting Parent and Brother Who is at hand. Now the long journey through the wastelands of illusion that we all willingly miscreated through fear and ignorance will terminate. All is accomplished forever, by our arrival Home "in no time."

Raymond Pratt
Samhain 2006

A Glossary of Terms

A COURSE IN MIRACLES: This is a book that has been scripted by Helen Shuckman and Bill Thetford and is changing how we literally see the world. It is a book that holds the key to the fastest way of returning home to Heaven.

ARCANA: This word pertains to the old English word, arcane or ancient, as in "arcane" secrets.

ATTACK: These are what would be perceived as unnecessary countermeasures taken by people who are fearful due to ego's machinations. It can also include what happens to the self when past fears and guilt are not released.

B.C.E.: The new abbreviation for B.C., Before the Common Era.

C.E.: The Common Era or A.D., Anno Domini. This nomenclature is now preferred to be a more inclusive abbreviation, especially for belief systems that are not based on common Christian beliefs.

COMPLETENESS: This is what we return to finally, the completeness of the Holy Trinity where we join with Yeshua, our Brother, as a part of the Second Person of the Holy Trinity.

EGO: Our creation of an ersatz or alter-god with whom we have originally given power to, through fear and confusion. Ego is fear incarnate.

FEAR: The negative emotion available to us that keeps us trapped within perceived existences and that extends out as a natural extension of guilt.

FORGIVENESS: The positive road needed to be taken to return to the Father. It is our only assignment that we need to fulfill through the Holy Spirit to finally remember what we really are.

GOD: The Supreme Being with whom we share our real existence on a higher level. God does not consider us apart from His Oneness but, because of ego and its pernicious "gift" of guilt to us, we do consider ourselves apart from Him. God merely sees His Holy Creations as temporarily asleep and dreaming of exile.

GUILT: This is a notion that was created by ego to keep us trapped in a thought system where we think we need to hide from God. Because we believe that we have done something distasteful in the Eyes of God, we fear retribution.

HOLY SPIRIT: This is our Voice or Remembrance of God, Who was created and extended out to us when we perceived our initial "loss" of Heaven. He is our quiet Mentor always waiting in the sidelines to help. For me, He is the Divine Compost Maker, for He takes all of the trash in our lives and puts it to good use.

HOLINESS: Holiness by definition has to be a little different to what we are used to. For instance, the holy man is a man who only sees holiness in his brother and sister. So holiness, in a sense, may have little or nothing to do with our worldly actions, but with how and what we correctly perceive.

HOLY INSTANT: A Holy Instant is a perceived point in time where, with the help of the Holy Spirit, we begin to recognize, even though it may be but for a very short moment, what we really are. It will usually entail seeing a brother or sister arrayed in all their heavenly beauty and majesty.

ILLUSION: We are unknowingly acting out those lives that we scripted a long time ago. The scenes are projected and are not real. We should be sitting behind the projector instead of pretending to play parts on the silver screen and considering it as something real.

LOVE & HEALING: This is what we must offer our brothers and sisters where there is a call for it. People who attack their brothers are really calling out for love. Love is the only positive emotion brought about by pure forgiveness.

MIND & THOUGHT SYSTEM: Our minds exist in two very distinct parts; one is very real and open to the Holy Spirit's incessant attempts to bring us back home. The lower mind created a world with ego, as a pale imitation of our real home and is, as such, constantly subject to ego's whims. The mind and thought system have only two choices, to either listen to our Mentor or to ego.

MIRACLE: This entails a shift of perception where one recognizes that all pain and suffering are not real but "gifts" from ego. With this acceptance by us from the Holy Spirit, miracles can happen easily for they define what is real and what is not. Miracles have no levels of performance difficulty; either something is perceived real or it is not.

MISCREATION: This word pertains to our faulty attempts at creating on this level. We are not supposed to create here but to heal and return. What we attempt to create outside of eternity is always subject to the laws of time and space, which are themselves a miscreation also.

PARACLETE: The word comes from the Greek word "para-kalein," which means to call on one to your side for assistance.

REAL & UNREAL: God's World is real and eternal. Ego's world is here on earth and, although shared by us, is unreal and subject to the limits of time and space. It will always remain a temporary outpost for us, but one that we can use as a steppingstone toward our eternal Reality.

SEPARATION: This is what keeps us longing for God. We perceive ourselves apart from Him because of "guilt." This guilt needs to be eradicated before going Home and is always accomplished by the actions of true forgiveness.

SONSHIP: This is the word used in *A Course in Miracles* to express our one, final, and Holy Union with Yeshua in the Second Person of the Holy Trinity. This is our Destiny.

SPECIAL RELATIONSHIPS: A holy relationship is one that embraces all mankind and seeks no reward; a special relationship, on the other hand, is considered as conditional for there is always a give and take in its makeup.

SPIRIT: What we ourselves and God in Heaven share throughout eternity.

TRIDENTINE MASS: This was the Catholic Latin Mass as used in churches worldwide and standardized a few centuries ago by the Council of Trent.It became obsolete after the Second Vatican Council.

YESHUA: This is the shortened Aramaic name for Jesus. It was originally spelled "Yeshushua" and can also be translated as the name Joshua. I use the Aramaic form to emphasize that our Brother, Yeshua, was not a Christian but a Jew and spoke Aramaic. Most probably, Yeshua spoke Hebrew, some Greek, and Latin; otherwise how could He have been able to talk to the Pharisees on the idiosyncrasies of Hebrew scripture? Or how would He have ever been able to answer the question, for that matter, asked of the Truth by Pontius Pilate? ("Quid est Veritas?" the Latin for "What is Truth?")

Raymond Pratt
Feabhra 2007

A Selection of Relevant Prayers

As we approach the end of this little edition, I have selected a number of what may be useful prayers to help us on our renewed journey home. I have used them for over a year and found them to be therapeutic and quite invaluable. To actually enjoy taking time out of my own busy life to pray, in general, hardly paints a true picture. But it has been particularly the case for me, and I tend to look forward to that time in prayer, more and more.

I do use all of these prayers that I have included on a regular basis and in conjunction with my own personal *A Course in Miracles* workbook. So I shouldn't be too surprised if, on application, after a short while, you find that your daily grind becomes quite more manageable. It may feel to you that you are a little more joyful, and that a smile and joke always seem to be ready to unfold from within like a blossoming flower.

Many people will notice the "new you" as it radiates outward like a homing beacon. It now also seems to you that they have finally lost that irritating edginess about them, and they will tend to feel more drawn to us and, indeed, us to them.

I do wish you all the very best in your endeavors. The way home is now a good deal more clearly marked, and I think we are now amply prepared for this, our final journey.

Whether we are hearing the quiet whisper urging us faithfully home, or mighty and strident blasts of the Holy Spirit's trumpet call, we watch and wait. In thankfulness, we remember what we were, as the walls and ramparts of our baseless fears and recriminations start to tumble down. We can now begin to build our new Jericho on the Holy Altar of Our Healing Mind. God be with you always!

THE NATURE OF GOD

There is only God, and God is.
    I am made in His Image,
I am simply Love.
    The Lord God is One and He is.
We are all made in His Image,
    We are all simply Love, God is.

FATHER IN HEAVEN

Father in Heaven, holy is Your Name.
    Yours is the Kingdom within me,
Yours is the Will done through me in the
    Now and forever.
Give us this day our Living Bread and
    Teach us to forgive and love
Our brothers and sisters,
    For You have always loved us.
Let us not be misled by the deceptions of ego
    And deliver us from all error.
Father, deliver us from all error, for were we not
    Created in Your Perfect Image, always innocent
And forever guilt-free?
    Remind us of our True Holiness by extending
Your never-ending Love through us, to all our
    Brothers and sisters still bound in exile, amen.

Raymond Pratt 2007

Today, God is in everything
    I think, feel, see, do, and say,
Because God is always in my mind.

THE MORNING PRAYER

What Truth, what Light thro' my Mind's window breaks?
It is the East, and the HOLY SPIRIT is the sun.
Arise, my Friend, dissolve the ego moon
Who is already sick and pale with grief
That You, the Truth are far more great than he.
Oh! It is the Christ child, yes it is my Love
And if I knew what I was, the brightness of my Mind
Would shame the stars as daylight does a lamp.
My Mind in Heaven would thro' the unseen regions
Stream so bright!
The world would sing and knoweth not the night.

William Shakespeare

THE ATONEMENT PRAYER

Holy Spirit!
    What I experience, I will make manifest.
If I am guiltless, I have nothing to fear.
    I choose to testify to my acceptance
Of the Atonement, not its rejection.
    I would accept my guiltlessness
By making it manifest and sharing it. Let me bring peace
    To God's Son from his Father.

A Course in Miracles

PRAYER OF SAINT FRANCIS OF ASSISI

Lord, make me an instrument of Your peace.
   Where there is hatred, let me sow Love.
Where there is injury, let me induce healing,
   Where there is doubt, let me instill faith,
Where there is despair, let me offer hope,
   Where there is darkness, let me shine Light
And where there is sadness, let me bring joy.
   O Divine Master, grant that I may not seek
So muchto be consoled, as to console;
   To be understood, as to understand;
To be loved, as to love;
   For it is in giving that we receive
And it is in forgiving
   That we are reborn into eternal Life.

SUBMISSION /RELEASE TO THE HOLY SPIRIT

I shall remember the Holy Presence of the One
Given to me to be the Source of judgment.
I shall give these to Him and say:
"Holy Spirit!
Take these from me and look upon them,
Judging them for me.
Let me not see them as a sign of sin and death,
Nor use them for destruction.
Teach me how NOT to make of them
An obstacle to peace, but
Let You use them for me, to facilitate their coming."

A Course in Miracles

HEALING THROUGH THE COURSE OF *MIRACLES*

I am here only to be truly helpful.
I am here to represent Him Who sent me.
I do not have to worry about what to say or
What to do, because He Who sent me will direct me.
I am content to be wherever He wishes,
Knowing He goes there with me.
I will be healed as I let Him teach me to heal.

I must have decided wrongly, because I'm
Not at peace.
I made the decision myself, but I can
Decide otherwise.
I want to decide otherwise, because I want
To be at peace.
I do not feel guilty, because the Holy Spirit
Will undo all consequences of my wrong decision
If I will let Him.
I choose to let Him, by allowing Him to decide
For God for me.

A Course in Miracles

PRAYER FOR EMPATHY WITH THE HOLY SPIRIT

I am not alone, and
I would not intrude the past upon my Guest.
I have invited Him, and He is here.
I need do nothing except, not to interfere!

PREREQUISITE TO FORGIVENESS PRAYER

Because I will to know myself,
I see you (NAME) as God's Son / Daughter
And my Brother / Sister.

THE MIRACLE OF FORGIVING

(NAME), you're not really there!
If I think you are guilty or the cause of the problem
And if I made you up,
Then the imagined guilt and fearmust be in me!
Since the separation from God has never occurred,
(NAME),
I forgive "both" of us for what we haven't done.
Now, there is only innocence and
I join with the HOLY SPIRIT in peace.

Course in Miracles

FORGIVENESS FROM *YOUR IMMORTAL REALITY*

Forgiving oneself:

I am immortal spirit,
This body is just an image,
It has nothing to do with what I am.

Forgiving one's brother/sister:

You are Spirit,
Whole and innocent,
All is forgiven and released.

From Gary Renard's *Your Immortal Reality*

MOTHER TERESA'S PRAYER TO YESHUA

Dear Yeshua, I believe you are the Son of God and
My Savior.
I need Your love to cleanse me from my errors.
I need Your light to drive away all darkness
.I need Your peace to fill and satisfy my heart.
I now open my heart and ask You to please enter
And let me receive Your gift of eternal Life.
Amen.

EXCERPTS FROM *A COURSE IN MIRACLES*

"When you perform a miracle, I will arrange both time and space to adjust to it. The miracle shortens time by collapsing it. This eliminates certain intervals within it. It does this within the larger temporal sequence."

"The body is the ego's idol; the belief in sin made flesh and then projected outward. This produces what seems to be a wall of flesh around the mind, keeping it prisoner in a tiny spot of space and time, beholden unto death, and given but an instant in which to sigh and grieve and die in honor of its master. And this unholy instant seems to be life; an instant of despair, a tiny island of dry sand, bereft of water and set uncertainly upon oblivion."

"You need not fear the Higher Court will condemn you. It will merely dismiss the case against you. There can be no case against a child of God and every witness to guilt in God's creations is bearing false witness to God Himself. Appeal everything you believe gladly to God's Own Higher Court, because it speaks for Him and therefore speaks truly. It will dismiss the case against you, however carefully you have built it up. The case may be fool-proof, but it is not God-proof. The Holy Spirit will not hear it because he can only witness truly. His verdict will always be thine is the Kingdom, because He was given to you to remind you of what you are."

"Any attempt to reinterpret sin as error is always indefensible to the ego. The idea of sin is wholly sacrosanct to its thought system, and quite unapproachable except with reverence and awe. It is the most 'holy' concept of the ego's system; lovely and powerful, wholly true, and necessarily protected with every defense at its disposal. For here lies its 'best' defense, which all the others serve. Here is its armor. Its protection and the fundamental purpose of the special relationship in its interpretation."

"There is no stone in all the ego's embattled citadel that is more heavily defended than the idea that sin is real; the natural expression of what the Son of God has made himself to be, and what he is. To the ego, there is no mistake. For this is its reality; this is the 'truth' from which escape will always be impossible. This is his past, his present and his future. For he has somehow managed to corrupt his Father, and change His Mind completely. Mourn, then, the death of God, Whom sin has killed! And this would be the ego's wish, which in its madness it believes it has accomplished.

Would you not rather that all this be nothing more than a mistake, entirely correctable, and so easily escaped from that its whole correction is like walking through a mist into the sun? For that is all it is. Perhaps you would be tempted to agree with the ego that it is far better to be sinful than mistaken. Yet think you carefully before you allow yourself to make this choice. Approach it not lightly, for it is the choice of hell or Heaven."

"The Thought of God surrounds your little kingdom waiting at the barrier you built to come inside and shine upon the barren ground."

"Within this kingdom the ego rules, and cruelly. And to defend this little speck of dust it bids you fight against the universe. This fragment of your mind is such a tiny part of it that, could you but appreciate the whole, you would see instantly that it is like the smallest sunbeam to the sun, or like the faintest ripple on the surface of the ocean. In its amazing arrogance, this tiny sunbeam has decided it is the sun; this almost imperceptible ripple hails itself as the ocean. Think how alone and frightened is this little thought, this infinitesimal illusion, holding itself apart against the universe. The sun becomes the sunbeam's 'enemy' that would devour it, and the ocean terrifies the little ripple and wants to swallow it.

Yet neither sun nor ocean is even aware of all this strange and meaningless activity. They merely continue, unaware that they are feared and hated by a tiny segment of themselves. Even that segment is not lost to them, for it could not survive apart from them. And what it thinks it is in no way changes its total dependence on them for its being. Its whole existence still remains in them. Without the sun the sunbeam would be gone; the ripple without the ocean would be inconceivable."

All seven entries in this chapter are excerpts taken from *A Course in Miracles*.

EXCERPTS FROM THE ST. THOMAS GOSPEL

These logia, of which a number have been inserted from the St. Thomas Gospel, come particularly close as to what we might imagine how the "Sayings Gospel," now lost, would look like. The logia originate from St. Thomas from about 40 to 50 C.E. and seem to possibly predate the three synoptic Gospels, which themselves stemmed from the Q or Quelle manuscript. The Quelle is thought, in all probability, to be the "Sayings Gospel" itself.

01: And He said, "Whoever discovers the interpretation of these sayings will not taste death."

05: "Know what is in front of your face, and what is hidden from you will be disclosed to you. For there is nothing hidden that will not be revealed."

11: "The dead are not alive, and the living will not die."

13: And He took him, and withdrew, and spoke three sayings to him. When Thomas came back to his friends, they asked him, "What did Yeshua say to you?" Thomas said to them, "If I tell you one of the sayings He spoke to me, you will pick up rocks and stone me, and fire will come from the rocks and consume you."

13a: "You dream of a desert, where mirages are your rulers and tormentors, yet these images come from you."

13b: "Father did not make the desert, and your home is still with him."

13c: "To return, forgive your brother, for only then do you forgive yourself."

18: The followers said to Yeshua, "Tell us how our end will be." He said, "Have you discovered the beginning then, so that you are seeking the end? For where the beginning is, the end

will be. Fortunate is the one who stands at the beginning:
That one will know the end and will not taste death."

22: "When you make the two into one, and when you make the
inner like the outer, and the outer like the inner, and the upper like the lower, and when you make male and female into
a single one, so the male will not be male and the female
will not be female…then you will enter the Kingdom."

26: "You see the speck that is in your brother's eye but you do
not see the log that is in your own eye. When you take the
log out of your own eye, then you will see clearly enough to
take the speck out of your brother's eye."

31: "A prophet is not acceptable in his own town. A doctor does
not heal those who know him."

36: "Do not worry, from morning to night and from night until
morning about what you will wear."

42: "Be passersby."

47: "A person cannot mount two horses or bend two bows. And
a servant cannot serve two masters, or that servant will
honor the one and offend the other."

49: "Fortunate are those who are alone and chosen, for you will
find the Kingdom. For you have come from it, and you will
return there again."

54: "Fortunate are the poor, for yours is the Father's Kingdom."

61: "I am the One who comes from what is Whole. I was given
from the things of My Father. Therefore, I say that if one is
whole, one will be filled with light, but if one is divided, one
will be filled with darkness."

94: "One who seeks will find. And for one who knocks, it shall be opened."

95: "If you have money, do not lend it at interest. Rather, give it to someone who will not pay you back."

108: "Whoever drinks from My Mouth shall become like Me. I, Myself, shall become that person, and the hidden things will be revealed to that person."

113: The disciples said to Him, "When will the Kingdom come?" He said, "It will not come by watching for it. It will not be said, 'Behold here' or 'Behold there.' Rather, the Kingdom of the Father is spread out upon the earth, and people do not see it."

These are excerpts from the Gospel of St. Thomas, and these are the hidden sayings that the living Yeshua spoke and Didymus Judas Thomas recorded. Found with the Nag Hammadi collection in Egypt, shortly after the Second World War, the full corrected logia can be seen in Gary Renard's *Your Immortal Reality*.

About the Author

Raymond Pratt was born in Nenagh, a small town of 5,000 souls, nestled in the bosom of the Slieve Arra and Silvermine mountains. It is tucked away in the north part of County Tipperary, in the Republic of Ireland. His late father, Samuel (Sam) Pratt, was an American aviator, an aerobatic pilot, and an aviation technician among other things, and was quite a well-known character around Shannon Airport. Sam was married to Raymond's mother, Marie O'Kane, who is Limerick born and bred.

Raymond received a comprehensive and classical Jesuit education throughout his formative years. First, at the now closed Crescent College in Limerick's city center, and then finally at Mungret College, a boarding school that was formerly open up to about 1972, and located on the city's western outskirts.

Weak eyesight would prevent him from following in his father's footsteps, and a profound wandering nature probably would have precluded it anyway. Three stints in the 27th Infantry Battalion based in Dundalk, the Irish Air Corps in Baldonnel, and the US armed forces in West Germany did not hinder this innate and overpowering wanderlust. It ultimately would find him and his young family living by the far-off South American shores of the Republic of Argentina. Raymond then engaged himself in teaching Keynesian economics in classes to private high-school students and taught the old Irish Gaelic language to whoever wished to learn.

Raymond had by now married an Argentine woman of German descent by the name of Cristina Cuerda de Stange in 1982 in Boston. They had met in the previous year, while working in the USA's capital, Washington DC. After almost 17 years together, where they lived mostly in southern Germany, Britain, Ireland,

Argentina, and the Salt Lake City area of Utah, they then sadly parted ways. The couple was truly blessed with six hale and hearty children, five boys and one girl.

Ciaran (The Dark One), the oldest of the five boys, is closely followed by Raymond's only daughter, Cristin, who suffers from a severe case of wanderlust also. There are also the four other younger sons, Brendan (Of the Navigator fame), Brian (Of the High King fame), Cathal (Battleworthy), and Conor (Houndlover), they are all presently living in Utah with their mother.

Raymond states that the roots of his first book took hold during the dark years soon after the divorce. While searching to put a meaning to an existence that was fast becoming devoid of a complete family life, he tried endlessly to cope. He states that it was, at times, very hard, for anti-depressive drugs were anathema and not a valid option for helping him.

Raymond has been happily working in Salt Lake City for the airlines for well over sixteen years now. He states that he will remain here, at least until Conor, his youngest child, reaches his majority, about five years hence.

The idea of writing this book was a very recent one for Raymond and he hopes that by finishing this edition it will be the sole measure by how he embraces his own personal success.

The book he has written *Beyond Forgotten Veils,* is quite important to him. For it is in its contents that he sees rewards that he hopes will pay off in huge spiritual dividends, not only for himself but for all students of the Course in Miracles. Books can be, and are generally seen by most authors as a novel way of entertaining and endorsing their own conception of immortality. They can, for that reason, carry a tremendous dividend, fully latent within any spiritually instructive edition, all into another perceived life. This is completely regardless of whether such a lifetime needs to be perceived again or not.

His book, he readily admits, is strongly based on the advanced forgiveness process that is inherent in a well-known spiritual book called *A Course in Miracles.* In it he sees that there are lessons to be taught and re-learnt for all. All of this, Raymond acknowledges, is something that may not have been possible to endorse and contribute toward if he was still married. It is for this reason alone, that Raymond is finally able to see the big picture which led him to forgiving all.

Readers, you have been presented with Raymond's first foray into the writer's world with the first edition of his instructive book Beyond Forgotten Veils. We hope that you have enjoyed it!

Printed in the United States
200906BV00003B/100-171/A